Whatcha Gonna Do If the Grid Goes Down?

Preparing Your Household For the Year 2000

© 1998, 1999 by Susan E. Robinson

All rights reserved. No part of this book may be reproduced, in any form or by any means, without written permission from the publisher.

Printed in the United States of America

Illustrations and Cover Design by Mark Stansell

Disclaimer: *This book was written for informational purposes only. The author and publisher will not be held accountable or liable in connection with the use of this book or the information herein. Information regarding sources and suppliers was as accurate as possible at the time of publication. This book does not contain lists of all possible suppliers. The author and publisher assume no responsibility for the availability or quality of products referenced in this book, or for the business practices of suppliers listed.*

All product names mentioned within the book are trademarks of their original owners.

The members of the Olsen family, their neighbors, and the town of Taylor Springs, Colorado are fictitious. Any resemblance they may have to actual persons or places is purely coincidental.

Published by:
Virtual Sage
PO Box 100008
Denver, CO 80250-0008
(303) 282-0708

ISBN 0-9667625-1-7

Whatcha Gonna Do If the Grid Goes Down?

Preparing Your Household For the Year 2000

By Susan Robinson

Illustrations and Cover Design by Mark Stansell

Virtual Sage

Published by Virtual Sage
Denver, Colorado

To Mr. Ted Rhodes

Acknowledgments

I would like to express my sincere thanks to all of the people who believed in this book, and who assisted me during the project. First, my highest regards and gratitude go to my editor and literary agent, Stephany Evans, for her enthusiasm, her belief in the book, her wisdom, and her unfailing support. Without her, this project would not have happened.

The team was blessed to have a most talented and dedicated artist, Mark Stansell. Thank you Mark, for your encouragement, your friendship, your perseverance, and your faith, as well as for your brilliant depiction of the Olsen family.

Many people were interviewed for this book, and answered my questions regarding writing and publishing. Thank you for taking time out of your busy schedules to give me guidance and professional advice.

Writing a book is primarily a solitary journey. The people who listened, believed, and provided emotional support were integral contributors to the project. Thanks to Tracey, Max, Karen, Dave, Mary, Ira, John, Grant, Eric, Sam, Tim, Ernie, Brian, Jim, Leslie, Cindy, Kristi, Susan, and Adam - dear friends who listened to theories about the Year 2000, coached me through the various phases of the project, bought me meals, and provided honest and supportive feedback. Thanks especially to my good friend Kay for her superior proofreading skills and constant encouragement.

Finally, this book is dedicated to Mr. Ted Rhodes. Mr. Rhodes and his wife Nadine have devoted much of their lives and their personal time to the Girl Scouts of America. I was privileged to know Mr. Rhodes when I was a teenager and a member of his Girl Scout troop. Many of my fondest memories are of the camping trips our troop took in Europe, Canada, and the Colorado Rockies. Learning from Mr. Rhodes and the scouts I met from all over the world has made a tremendous impact in my life. It is ironic to me, twenty three years after I last saw Mr. Rhodes, that the Girl Scout motto, "Be Prepared," and the lessons he taught me (with his tactful suggestions and wonderful sense of humor) about my own strengths and ability to do whatever I put my mind to, have provided the foundation on which this work is built.

Table of Contents

Acknowledgments .... *vii*
Table of Contents .... *ix*
Preface .... *xi*
Index *141*

CHAPTER 1: WHY WORRY? 13

FIRST STEPS 15
THE MANUAL 15
JANUARY 1, 2000 - THE WAY IT MIGHT BE. 16
JANUARY 1, 2000 - THE WAY IT CAN BE. 17
    Anne's Action Plan 19

CHAPTER 2: LIFE WITHOUT THE GRID 21

WORKING TOGETHER 21
YOUR MONEY OR YOUR LIFE 23
GOT ANY GOOD IDEAS? 23
    Y2K Expectations 26
    Kitchen Supply Worksheet 31
    Bathroom Supply Worksheet 35
    First Aid Kit Worksheet 39
    Critical Electronic Devices Worksheet 43
    Battery Inventory Worksheet 47
    Games and Entertainment Worksheet 51
    General Household Action Plan 53

CHAPTER 3: FOOD STORAGE 55

GETTING A FIX ON OUR FOOD HABITS 55
HAVE IT YOUR WAY 56
    Level 1 Basics for Family of Four 57
    Menu Planner 61
    Level 1 Shopping Planner 67
DO'S AND DON'TS 70
    Level 1 Food Storage Menus 75
    Level 1 Shopping List 77
    Sources for Preparedness Food 85
    Level 1 Food Storage Action Plan 87
LEVEL 2 FOOD STORAGE PREPAREDNESS 89
LEVEL 3 FOOD STORAGE PREPAREDNESS 91

CHAPTER 4: WATER BASICS 93

WATER STORAGE 94
SOURCES OF WATER 95
WATER PURIFICATION 96
    Water Purification Alternatives 97
    Sources for Water Storage and/or Purification Supplies 98
    Water Action Plan 99

CHAPTER 5: FOOD PREPARATION 101
- COOKING WITHOUT ELECTRICITY 102
- STOVES 104
- OVENS 106
- COOKWARE 106
- LIVING WITHOUT A REFRIGERATOR 108
- ROOT CELLARING, DRYING, AND CANNING 108
- TO GRIND OR NOT TO GRIND 109
  - *Food Preparation Supplies - Mail Order Sources* *111*
  - ***Food Preparation Action Plan*** *113*

CHAPTER 6: LIGHT, HEAT, WASHING, AND WASTE 115
- LET THERE BE LIGHT 116
- SHELTER FROM THE COLD 118
- GARBAGE IN - GARBAGE OUT 120
- CLEANING UP THE KITCHEN 121
- LIFE WITHOUT THE LOO 122
- LOW-TECH LAUNDRY 123
  - *Light, Heat, Washing, and Waste Supplies - Mail Order Sources* *125*
  - *Light and Heat Action Plan* *127*
  - *Washing and Waste Action Plan* *129*
  - ***Light, Heat, Washing, Waste Blank Action Plan*** *131*

CHAPTER 7: TAKING ACTION 133
- HOW TO STAGE A BACK-TO-BASICS WEEKEND 134
- WHAT WE'VE LEFT OUT 136
  - ***Year 2000 Final Action Plan*** *139*

Preface

People write books for many reasons. I wrote this book because I realized that *someone* must write it. Really. It was that simple.

It all started on February 28, 1998. It was an ordinary Saturday. I was flying from San Diego to Denver to spend time with my family over the weekend before wrapping up a consulting project on Monday. Several years before, I had moved from Colorado to San Francisco to open a consulting practice. My specialty was strategy integration - marketing, systems, and operations - supporting the telecommunications industry.

I have a twenty year background in computers, experience born out of necessity and coincidence, rather than choice. Basically, I was too clumsy to waitress in college. I couldn't carry all of those plates and drinks. But, I could type fast, and I was a future-oriented person. The industry needed computer operators and keypunch people, and paid better than other part-time jobs. So, I began as a keypuncher, then I worked my way up to data center operations, MIS architecture, systems design, and eventually to full blown IT consultant.

Throughout my career, I experienced the evolution of the adoption of computers. One of my jobs was to interview people about how they performed their jobs, document the manual processes, and then use the information to design a computer to do similar tasks. I helped people progress from typewriters to word processors, word processors to personal computers. I observed how they made the transition. This skill helped me to see and understand the links between people, processes, and automated systems.

Now, back to the airplane. On February 28, I met someone who would provide me with information that would drastically change my life and my focus - almost immediately. He was a rather ordinary looking, fifty-something man. Not someone I would notice in a crowded room, or even someone I would seek out. We started with small talk, about traveling in general, losing luggage, etc. Before the flight attendants even presented the security announcement, we were involved deeply in a conversation about computer infrastructure.

I'm not sure how we arrived at the subject, I think I brought it up first. I told him I'd just moved from San Francisco to San Diego, and that it had taken more than twenty telephone conversations to transfer my health insurance from California Region 01 to California Region 04, and to change my primary care physician. I said "I think the computer infrastructure in this country is broken." And he said, "You know, it's funny you mention that because I know a physician in San Diego who is convinced that in the Year 2000, the majority of the technological infrastructure in the world is going to stop working." He went on to explain that this doctor had quit practicing medicine for two years to try to warn people that the food supply, public utilities, health care, etc. would be impaired.

It made sense to me. To make a long story short, I met the physician, read his research, and did my own investigating. I reached the same conclusion. The information highway we depend on in the United States to provide us with water, heat, food, transportation, and electricity is in serious jeopardy. The so-called Y2K millennium bug will not be fixed completely, and there will be consequences. I believed (and still believe) that most people will be without electricity, natural gas, running water, and food - for at least a month, and maybe longer - beginning on January 1, 2000 - in the middle of winter.

While many books have been written about what might happen, I couldn't find a book about what to do in one's own household to cope with this particular situation. And, I knew, that without preparation, there would be chaos. It was almost like a premonition. I would write this book on how to survive. Someone needs to write it, why not me, moí, a person who is not an expert - not even a novice when it comes to food storage, renewable energy, or self-sustaining life styles.

I decided that if I could learn and prepare myself, then anyone can learn. I created the fictitious Olsen family, and their suburban Denver neighborhood of Taylor Springs, to represent the day-to-day lifestyle of a typical American family. Through their characters, I was able create pictures and stories instead of mere instructions.

Welcome to the second edition of the book. Since the first edition was published, only three short months ago, I have developed relationships with wonderful preparedness product vendors, and discovered some new and valuable products. The fictional text, and the story of the Olsen family has barely changed. The Mail Order Source Lists have changed ever so slightly. If you own the first edition, then you probably don't need this one.

This is a miracle book. I am a first time author. The book was written in only six months, and published on a schedule that many would call completely insane. The book exists because it was destined to exist. It has developed a following since the initial publication that is phenomenal. Even though it was written for the suburban soccer mom who hadn't started preparing, men love this book - and, surprisingly - veteran survivalists have told me they are using it in their own homes because the book contains so much information they haven't thought of. After only ten weeks on the Internet at Amazon.com, *Whatcha Gonna Do...?* ranked in the top 200 in sales. My sincere thanks go to all of you who continue to support this book at a grass roots level by either reselling it, or by telling your friends and neighbors about it.

Before concluding, I must comment on the increase of "gloom and doom" information and sensationalists who are writing books and prophesying the end of society as we know it. Ignore them. I do. They don't believe in you. They think they must put you into panic mode in order to persuade you to take action and prepare your household. Most of these people have decided to relocate to the middle of nowhere. Many of them are famous. Realize that they have a different decision to make than you do. Some of the preparedness experts feel vulnerable, and are concerned the unprepared masses may show up on their doorsteps if they don't relocate. Their concern is legitimate; their approach is not. Understand that what we collectively will to happen in the year 2000 - be it positive or negative, is what WILL happen.

The Year 2000 infrastructure failure, even if it is only a few weeks long, provides us with tremendous opportunity. We will understand the value of our family and friends as part of our preparedness team. We will know that whatever garbage and pollutants we create will end up, literally - in our own back yard. We will rediscover books, and create our own perceptions through imagination, instead of being fed them by television. We will teach our children that one person can make a difference, and that because they are here with us, they are an integral part of their family's future. Our talents and lives will now have instantly redeemable value, as we realize the benefits of hard work to be the ability to have warm shelter and food on the table. We will worry about the things that really matter - relationships, the ecosystem of our planet, and our innate abilities as humans to innovate and to overcome challenges. We will be grateful for everything we ever had, and everything we will have again.

It is my sincere hope that everyone who reads this book will see that, like the Olsen family, we all have the potential to reduce the severity of whatever happens on January 1, 2000.
Y2K - We will find a way...

Susan Robinson
Denver, Colorado
January, 1999

Why Worry?

My name is Nancy Olsen. And, I'm one of the lucky ones. When you hear about my life, you'll think it's fairly ordinary. I have a husband named Al and two kids. Ben is ten years old and Katie is five. We live in Taylor Springs, Colorado, a rapidly growing suburb south of Denver. We're a typical, average, middle-of-the-road kind of family with a three bedroom house and a golden retriever named Cisco. What makes us special is that we have a strategy. Well, we have more than a strategy. We have a tactical plan for disaster recovery - plus the tools we need, just in case. Our family decided to prepare for the Year 2000. That's why I'm so lucky.

It all started on February 28, 1998, a typical Saturday morning - cartoons blaring, laundry basket overflowing, Al oblivious and reading the paper, Cisco barking (like a dog possessed) at the cat next door. I'm flipping half-burned pancakes, Ben's sitting at the kitchen table putting on rollerblades (and not waiting for breakfast) - and the phone rings. Ben leaps across the room to answer the phone, scratching and scraping tile as he drags his skate. "Mom, it's for you - it's Aunt Annie." Welcome to our weekend in paradise.

My sister Anne maintains a serene existence based on the key elements of leisurely reading, organic food, mood lighting, eclectic music, and total independence. No one has ever thrown up in her house, and she has an anxiety attack if she finds a dog hair on her slacks. She is a thirty-seven year old technical librarian, unmarried, no kids. Her idea of stress is when she's taking care of my kids and one of them spills a glass of milk at the dinner table. Every once in a while, I sneak into the back of my walk-in closet, close my eyes, and pretend I live at Anne's house. I don't think she ever wishes she lived at mine.

"What's going on? I thought you were going to Vail this weekend," I said.

Chapter 1 — Why Worry?

"Oh, I was going to, but I read an interesting book this week, and it kind of made me think. I decided not to spend the money."

"Was it a self-help book?" I asked, smirking.

"No, it was a book about the Year 2000 computer crisis," she replied. Anne went on to explain that the book, written by respected computer software guru, Ed Yourdon and his daughter, Jennifer, was called *Time Bomb 2000: What the Year 2000 Computer Crisis Means to You*![1]

"The basic premise of the book is that the millennium bug situation has serious implications. The Yourdons suggest the problem is too complex and immense to solve, and predicts disruption of public utilities, food distribution, financial institutions, etc. They also say that people should be prepared to survive without electricity, water, and access to food for at least a month. The depth and reach of the problem are also tough to assess. I think we'd better do some research. I'm not spending money on anything that doesn't contribute to my survival - at least until I figure out how real this thing is."

Did I mention that my sister Anne is the most self-sufficient person I know? She was in Girl Scouts until her junior year in high school, and I think their motto, "Be Prepared," is secretly tattooed somewhere on her body. Anne is the only person I know who sleeps in leggings and a big T-shirt when she travels ("Just in case there is a fire in the hotel,"). She keeps a flashlight by her bed (with fresh batteries), and counts the number of rows to the nearest exit on airplanes. Had she been on the Titanic, she would have figured out there weren't enough life rafts, and left the ship before it sailed. People fight to have her on their team in those management training classes where you pretend you're preparing for a survival hike, and you only can take 60% of the stuff with you in your backpack.

Usually, because of that sibling rivalry thing - I disagree with Anne, try to argue with her, and resist her compulsion to anticipate every possibility and control every situation. But, for some reason, this time, I just stood there.

"Nancy?"

"I'm here. How do we check this thing out?"

"I'm going to spend some time on the Web this morning. I'll call you back."

Well, as they say, the rest is history. Anne did her research, and even though we kept thinking - this really isn't going to happen, it's unbelievable, it's inconceivable - we trusted our instincts, and put every extra dollar and ounce of spare energy we had - into our preparation for the Year 2000.

At first, when Anne started showing me statistics about the sheer number of computers, the wishy-washy responses and quotes from car makers, the government, public utility workers, banks, etc. - I kind of freaked out. I had nightmares. I couldn't sleep. I didn't know if I should tell people. And then, coincidentally, I was talking to one of my friends who is an environmentalist, and he told me how he starts the discussion with people about global warming, if it is really happening, and the potential consequences.

> "What if you were going to get on an airplane this afternoon, and when you got to the airport, the airline told you that there was a 10% chance that the airplane would crash, and you would be killed? Would you get on the plane? Probably not. What if they told

---

[1] Yourdon, Edward and Yourdon, Jennifer. *Time Bomb 2000: What the Year 2000 Computer Crisis Means to You.* New Jersey, Prentice-Hall, 1998.

Chapter 1 — Why Worry?

you there was a 5% chance the plane would crash? Would you get on the plane? Probably not, still." Then, you ask the person, "Do you think there is at least a 5% chance that I am right that global warming is a reality and that it could be seriously endangering our planet?"

I started thinking about the example from my own perspective. Would I get on the plane with a 5 or 10% chance of a crash? Probably not. Would I put my children on that plane? NO WAY! Well, if you think about the above scenario in the context of the Year 2000 situation, if there is only a 5% chance that the experts predicting widespread disruptions are correct, then I am on that plane. My kids are on that plane. And so is anyone who is dependent on an integrated infrastructure based on information technology to sustain their existence. Even though we have made more progress than any nation in fixing the bug, the United States is especially vulnerable. If you live in a "highly developed" nation, you got it - you are on that plane, too.

First Steps

Fortunately, you are reading these words. You have already taken the first step to preparing for the Year 2000. While many books have been written about emergency preparedness, they tend to be very specialized and complicated. Me, I'm the queen of simplicity. I can't just take a hiatus from my jobs as a part-time writer and full-time domestic engineer and do everything these books tell you to do. I need an easier plan. So, I decided to keep a diary about what we did in the Olsen family, and eventually, it became this book.

When we started preparing, we realized that several factors enter into how to proceed: 1) Where you live, 2) How much discretionary money you have, 3) How many people live in your household, 4) How much you are willing to depend on other people (the government, etc.) to take care of you if things are disrupted, 5) How much spare time you have to spend on the effort, and 6) When you finally hear about this and how much time is left until 1/1/2000.

Obviously, we couldn't possibly cover every situation. So, this book is written from the perspective of a family of four living in a single family home in a Denver, Colorado suburb. For most families, our scenarios will provide a model to start with. We have included strategies and alternative solutions for urban dwellers. If you live in a desert, or a townhouse in the suburbs, you may need to make modifications to our solutions. If you have infants toddlers or family members with special health needs, you will also need to adjust our recommendations. No matter where you live, if you simply do some of the things we suggest, you will probably be much better off than you are today.

The Manual

Let's talk a little bit about how we organized the book, and why. We started out with the basic assumption that the public utility grid - that massive infrastructure that provides you with electricity, natural gas, water, and dial tone - will fail on 1/1/2000. We hope it only fails for a few days, we suspect it will fail for a month, and we have considered it could fail for several months. So, *Chapter 2* talks about things to consider in general for coping with a temporary loss of public utilities. *Chapter 3* talks about how to plan for, buy, and store food for at least a month, and for longer if you wish. *Chapter 4* is dedicated to storing, purifying, and obtaining water. *Chapter 5* is dedicated to preparing and preserving food without electricity. *Chapter 6* gives instructions and suggestions related to day-to-day household management including lighting, heating, washing, cleaning, and sanitation. *Chapter 7* tells you how to take action and how to help you sharpen your

Chapter 1 — Why Worry?

coping skills by staging back-to-basics weekends, during which, your household will learn to live without electricity.

In each chapter, we have a scenario about what might happen or how we did our planning, major categories of things to consider, then lists of what types of supplies you should have in your house. We've also included sources about where to get them, a few general price estimates, and checklists to keep track of what you've done. We provide recommendations for three different levels of contingency preparation in each category. Level 1 is for people who aren't really convinced of a grid failure, but who want to have a few extra supplies, and be prepared for a one month grid failure or serious disruption of public utility services (everyone should do this). Level 2 is for people who accept there is a strong possibility of a grid failure, and who don't want to sacrifice basic comfort or inconvenience their families unnecessarily (most people can do this). Level 3 is for people who believe the problem will be bigger than anticipated, who don't want to be impacted hardly at all, and who are willing to spend a great deal of money and time to ensure against possible infrastructure failure. In response to every situation we examined, we found lots of neat products and solutions, but realized that everyone will have their own resource limitations.

For example, if we were talking about water preparedness as a category: Level 1 would include water storage and a purification system. Level 2 might include more water storage, portable containers, and a simple rainwater retention system (like gutter drains and a horse trough). Level 3 would include all of the above, plus a backup purification system, plus building a pond or cistern for storage. Our family is mostly in the Level 2 category of preparedness. You may find that you are at Level 1 in some categories, and want to go to Level 3 for others. One approach to getting closer to the maximum preparedness level, which we highly encourage, is to work with your neighbors. If your neighbors are prepared, they probably won't be bothering you to provide for them. For some of the tools in the Level 3 category, you may be able to have a few items in your neighborhood, and share.

We think we have an extremely talented family. I love to cook and garden. My husband Al is Mr. Fix It. He worked for his dad's construction company in college. And, I would pit my sister Anne against any military logistics officer on the planet when it comes to lists and organizational ability. So, we collaborated. We all read books, interviewed experts, and relied on our own strengths and skills to come up with practical and usable solutions.

In each chapter of the book, we try to make things as interesting and easy to follow as possible. We did our best to find good, reliable sources, products, and tips. We also recommend several books you can read on your own. We went to trade shows, looked at stores and products, searched the Worldwide Web, and read all of the books we refer to. As with any advice you get, we encourage you to do your own research and evaluations if you can. We cannot assume any liability, nor do we guarantee the performance of any of the things we tell you about. Also, these products and sources do not represent a comprehensive list of what is available. Now, we've covered the liability issues. Let's start with a little scenario.

January 1, 2000 - The way it might be.

If we woke up in our house on 1/1/2000, and if it was equipped the way it was on 2/28/98 - we would be in deep yogurt. The electricity is off, and it is snowing. I can't tell what time it is because the screen on my digital clock radio is dark and dead. When I pick up the telephone to call my sister, no dial tone. Al turns on the water faucet in the master bathroom - nothing. He goes downstairs to turn off the water to the house to prevent contamination, and to try to find buckets to drain the hot water heater into so we can save some drinking water. Ben has already flushed one toilet, so we just lost 7 gallons of potable water from the tank. I go to the basement to try to find

Chapter 1 — Why Worry?

the camping cooler to put the freezer stuff in. Al suggests we fill the cooler with refrigerator stuff, and put the freezer food in the snow.

Our next door neighbor comes over to tell us the utility company is forecasting a minimum two week outage of electricity and water. They have an AM radio with batteries. His wife walked to the grocery store (snowplows aren't operating), and said the police were there to let two people at a time in. Since the ATM's are down, and she only had $20 in cash, she couldn't get much. The drinking water is already sold out. She managed to get two packs of batteries and some soup.

We did an inventory of our possessions and realized that we had three flashlights. One needs C batteries, which we don't have. We have AA batteries for one flashlight. If we get out the Christmas stuff, we have about ten candles in the house. Our gas burning fireplace doesn't work, and we don't have any wood. We have about a half a tank of propane for our barbecue grill, and a camp stove with about 2 hours worth of gas left.

Our food supply is pretty good. We have macaroni and cheese, soup, refried beans, tortillas, pasta, chips, etc. We'll probably be okay for a week. Since our family skis, we have long underwear, wool sweaters, and good coats and hats. We only have ten cans of dog food, and three rolls of toilet paper. Breakfast is cold cereal with the last of the milk. The house is getting colder, and the kids are complaining about no television.

Does this sound like your house? We think it is pretty typical of what most people have around. Fortunately, we are prepared. Now, the Olsen family scenario, after investing a little time and money, looks so much better.

January 1, 2000 - The way it can be.

We wake up, and the house is still fairly warm. We added extra fiberglass insulation last summer, installed storm windows, and put up our thermal window coverings yesterday. Al lit a few cans of heating fuel in a portable fire pit, and placed it in the family room to generate a little more warmth. We have wind up clocks on all the bedsides, and kerosene lamps in the major living spaces. Each person in our family has their own small flashlight, and we have a solar battery charger and rechargeable batteries. Al is draining the hot water heater into 5 gallon water carriers, and dumping the water into a plugged bathtub. Ben is salvaging water from the toilet tanks (not bowls), and dumping them in the bathtub. He used the portable toilet we put in his bathroom last night, and since we converted to low water usage toilets, we will evaluate our water situation and decide how we will use indoor toilets, portables, and the outhouse (hole dug last summer before the ground froze). Since we all slept in long underwear, we didn't wake up freezing. Katie, who sleeps through everything, is still snoring.

I go downstairs and organize the ingredients for breakfast. In the basement, I fill my large, copper kettle with water from our 440 gallon drinking water reserve, using a pump installed in the lid. Later, I'll have Al fill one of the portable, 5 gallon water containers and bring it upstairs. I start to boil water for coffee. My French press coffee maker doesn't require electricity. Al finished draining the water heater, and started up his 1975 four-wheel-drive pickup - without an internal computer - to drive over to pick up Anne at 9:30, as we had prearranged. I whip up a batch of pancakes using powdered milk, powdered eggs, and flour from my food reserve. I cook them on a cast iron griddle on my propane camp stove, along with some frozen breakfast sausage. Fortunately, I practiced cooking on this stove during our preparedness weekend practices we held once a month during the last nine months. We had drills so we could learn how to live without electricity and running water. I also stir up some powdered butter for the top of the pancakes, and get some honey out of storage. Since we've already emptied our refrigerator, we just transfer our

Chapter 1 — Why Worry?

freezer stuff to coolers out in the snow. I mixed some powdered milk last night in a liquid storage container and put it in our insulated portable cooler with some ice packs.

The kitchen is warm, coffee is made, and everyone shows up for pancakes at 10:00. Katie comes down dressed in silk long underwear, a turtleneck, polypropylene pants, wool blend socks, and down booties. Everyone washes their hands in a wash basin with warm water. Al empties the wash basin in the water disposal hole we dug before the ground froze. We review our action plan and assignments for the conversion to temporary life without "the grid." Even though we're shocked and disappointed, we're very relieved that we have the things we need to live comfortably until our food supply and utilities are restored. Listening to our battery powered AM radio, we are saddened to hear that looting of hardware and grocery stores has begun, and people are cutting down trees in parks and common areas.

Chapter 1 — Why Worry?

Anne's Action Plan

Level 1	Level 2	Level 3
1. Accept the fact that the grid may go down or that utility service may be disrupted for a short time. Be willing to prepare for a month long failure.	1. Prepare to be without the grid for three months, and without access to groceries for six months.	1. Prepare to survive without the grid for six months and without access to a grocery store for one year.
2. Add preparedness as a line item to your monthly budget. Brainstorm as a family on ways to save or earn more money to devote to the effort. Commit to reducing waste in your family - food, money, clothing.	2. Take some money out of savings and have a garage sale. Redo the family budget, and place reductions from other categories in a special preparedness budget and schedule.	2. Devote discretionary spending to preparing for grid failure until the activity is complete.
3. Use the Action Plans in each chapter to complete the Level 1 activities.	3. Complete the Level 2 activities in each chapter. Assign different family members to be in charge of specific activities. Develop specific dates for completion. Plan to be fully prepared on or before June 1, 1999.	3. Complete the Level 3 activities in each chapter. Focus on preparedness whenever you have discretionary time. Organize efforts at work, church, and in your neighborhood to help others prepare.

Life Without the Grid

Working Together

Since the Olsen family heard about the potential consequences of the Year 2000 computer situation, we've felt fortunate. We realize this advance warning gives us an opportunity to figure out what to do and to take action, and we think that if we help others do the same, things will work out. Sounds simple doesn't it?

At first, I must admit, we questioned whom to tell. What would people think of us? Would we lose our friends, our professional reputations, the respect of others? Putting it in perspective, we realized those things were not the issue. What was significant was that we had knowledge that could help people, and we needed to share it indiscriminately.

When we first started telling our family, colleagues, and friends that we were writing a book about how to prepare for a potential grid shutdown, we were met with various reactions. Some people understood right away. Some thought we were being a little paranoid. Others moved back and forth between acceptance and denial, depending on what news story they had read the day before.

As we began conducting research for our project, we were very surprised that religion was such a prominent topic in the conversations we had with various experts and organizers of the

Chapter 2 — Life Without the Grid

preparedness movement. It wasn't surprising to learn that individuals of various religious backgrounds are actively working on emergency preparedness. We were caught off guard, however, when eventually, almost everyone we spoke with who is instrumental in the movement, asked what our personal convictions were. We understood that these people believed that their religion was the only path to salvation, and they wanted to make sure we would be protected. So, they approached and questioned us with good intentions. We have become increasingly concerned, however, that as the millennium approaches, religious affiliation may become a significant factor in determining how individuals cooperate with each other.

Throughout history, when people have faced challenging times, they have tended to focus on their differences, and have divided themselves according to race, nationality, and religion. As we attempt to bring preparedness into the mainstream, we find that some people want us to have a label so they can decide how to respond to our suggestions. Are we Mormon, Christian, New Age? While we are members of an organized religion, that affiliation is secondary to that fact that we're simply human. And, we happen to be American. If we need to fit into a category, I guess you could call us concerned and determined.

We are writing this book because we believe that collectively - all of us working together in our neighborhoods and our communities, will find a way to prepare for the future. The multi-cultural mix in the United States is one of our nation's greatest strengths. One example of how diversity helped us with this book is in our food chapter. When we looked at the preparedness books on the market, we realized that most of them provide food storage and recipes that are mainly traditional American or European. Most contain many recipes for bread, and recommend storing and using large quantities of flour and wheat. We spoke with our friends who are Chinese, Middle Eastern, and Mexican, to name a few, and realized that eating foods like rice and couscous, cooking in a wok, preparing dal, naan, tortillas, and stir-fried vegetables would add variety, be nutritious, and potentially make food preparation easier.

Our research also showed us how much we have in common with families who practice many different religions. When we visited with Jews, Mormons, Christians, Pagans, and those who classified themselves as "none of the above," we learned that every one of us agreed on the basics - if the grid goes down for a while, we want as many people as possible to have food, water, and warm shelter. No one knows what is really going to happen as a result of the Year 2000 computer glitch. But, we can't lose by taking precautions. We can eat the food we store; we will eventually save money and natural resources by investing in alternative energy products; and we can always use camping and first aid equipment. As a bonus, we'll also be prepared in case one of the increasingly frequent weather disasters decides to visit our town.

A few optimistic souls have "joked" that they didn't see any reason to prepare, because if Americans experience food shortages, they will just go into the streets with guns and steal the food from those who have it. The Olsen's philosophy is that the more advance preparation that occurs, the less negative consequences there will be. We acknowledge that there are fatalistic, scary, destructive people in this world. But, none of us wants to be in a position of having to take a gun and go to our neighbor's house to get food for our family, and we don't think that others want to be in that position, either. Through a collective focus on the positive, we can minimize the probability of these type of occurrences.

Another small matter surfaced when we began sharing our emergency plans and vision. We were advised to prepare in secret, and not to tell anyone what we were doing, giving our family an edge. The reality is that here in suburban Taylor Springs, we live about ten feet away from our next door neighbors. We can observe the activities in at least twenty houses near us. Besides, we kind of like these people. We'd really like to see them live long and healthy lives. Together, we are a resourceful group of people who can benefit from each other, and share our collective knowledge and talents. United we stand...

Chapter 2 — Life Without the Grid

Your Money or Your Life

When Al and I first started thinking about things like the fallibility of computers, as well as the dramatically increasing number of weather related disasters - it became obvious that we'd been living in a world of misplaced value. Our life had been happening on a treadmill - get up in the morning, make breakfast, hustle everyone off to work and school, then do the after-school rush for sports and meetings and dinner. Weekends were another balancing act consisting of rushing and scheduling. Throughout all of this, we happily spent money and consumed products. If something broke, we threw it away or donated it to charity, and then went out and bought a new one.

Our finances went to things like food, entertainment, trinkets for our house, toys for the whole family, bigger televisions, electronic games, compact discs, lots of new clothes, newer cars, jewelry, etc. We were a little stunned to realize that - except for food and a few camping supplies and ski clothes, none of the things we have spent money on for most of our lives will contribute to our ability to survive in an emergency.

As we started budgeting for food storage, tools that don't require electricity, and new insulation for our house, etc., we were embarrassed and actually repentant for our previously selfish and wasteful ways. I remember my grandmother, who had lived through the Great Depression and World War II. When she moved out of her house of eighteen years, she had many canning supplies, tools, hardware, wind-up clocks, and things that had been repaired, mended, and reused. We gave most of her possessions to charity, but in the end, we just threw some items away so we could finish the overwhelming chore of cleaning out her house. Back then, we didn't consider the waste. Why would we want an old pan with a taped handle when we could just go out and buy a new one? Most of our generation and our children's generation don't know what it is like to "do without." This is a lesson we may have a chance to learn.

When Al and I decided to redirect much of our saving and investing money to our emergency activities, and to actually sell stock to prepare more quickly, we discussed it with our friends. Most of the people we know said they would have a difficult time even considering reducing their market investments. Some said they had reluctantly reorganized their stock portfolio by eliminating some high-tech companies and then investing in camping product and solar equipment manufacturers. That made them feel better about their preparedness for the future.

It continues to amaze us how willing people in the US are to pay hundreds of dollars a month for health insurance and car insurance just in case something happens, but when we started suggesting to our friends and family that they divert much of their discretionary spending to purchase water storage and purification systems, food storage, canning supplies, and gardening tools - they looked at us like we were crazy. Many of them couldn't conceive of voluntarily lowering their standard of living today to prepare for a potential infrastructure failure that would occur months from now. Maybe it is because our environment in the US has been stable for so long. I can't say I've ever gone to the grocery store and not been able to find at least some brand of an item I wanted. We've all lived the good life. It's hard to imagine anything so "third world" happening here. But, as public awareness increases, we hope that preparing in case of emergency will become as natural as buying homeowner's insurance. We hope it happens soon, very soon.

Chapter 2 — Life Without the Grid

Got Any Good Ideas?

Before we started actually planning and prioritizing our Year 2000 activities, we decided to think about how our lives might change during a grid failure. We also wanted to get our kids to start thinking about it, so if it does occur, they will already know about what to expect. The adults in our family decided that we will start implementing lifestyle changes immediately. The more of our behavior we change now, the less adjustment will be required in the future.

We wanted to try to make the planning activity fun, and to include the kids. So, we invited Anne over, ate some pizza, got out a few notepads, and started brainstorming about how things might be different, and what we could start doing now to adjust.

The rules of brainstorming, as you team management geeks know, is that no answer is a bad answer, and that everything someone thinks of is written down to motivate new thoughts. The goal of brainstorming is to create possibilities, not to evaluate how realistic they might be.

Our kids turned out to be masters at anticipating the consequences.

"No TV, no video games, no computer, no fun," moaned Ben.

"Thank you, Mr. Optimism," said Anne.

"No McDonald's?" asked Katie.

"Actually, no fast food," says Al. "This is going to be great."

"And we don't know if everyone will be able to go to school or work initially. So, we should plan on having enough food for at least a month, to feed everyone in the family three meals a day - seven days a week - entirely from what we have in the house," says Anne, matter-of-factly.

"No school? Cool." Ben is now beaming.

"Really, if we're totally prepared, we will assume no access to any kind of stores," I said.

"First positive, huge savings when you guys can't shop," smirks my lovely husband.

"What about garbage?" The neat freak Anne is already thinking about cleanliness.

"Trash pickup could be temporarily disrupted, also. We might as well assume that everything we would normally throw away will have to either be burned or be buried in the backyard."

We realized right away after having this discussion that our consume, throw away, and buy more pattern really must change to properly manage the situation. So, we thought about some things we could do to minimize the waste problem.

"Okay," said Anne. "What about if we use different colored bandannas instead of paper napkins. Each person has a different color. We can reuse them for several meals, and then hand wash or wash in the non-electric washer. They will also hang dry quickly."

My sister is so darn brilliant. We realized we could also use dishrags and thin cotton dishtowels instead of sponges and paper towels. And that we definitely want to store environmentally friendly dish soap and cleaning supplies. Oh, bandannas can also be used instead of paper tissues. It is

Chapter 2 — Life Without the Grid

amazing how our perspective changes when it is <u>literally</u> our own back yard that we're putting our trash in. Also, the less space we use to store paper products, the more space we have for food and other essentials.

"We might as well just start changing our behavior right away. No more sponges, and we'll try to use less paper towels. I'll put bandannas on the shopping list," I said.

"We should also buy food or store food in containers that can be washed, and try to minimize packaging. Less waste. More space."

"Do you realize how much food we throw away in this house?" said Al. "We need to really figure out how much each person eats, and prepare only that much at each meal. It will be difficult to store and dispose of leftovers. Oh, and we need to compost stuff that would normally go down the garbage disposal."

"No TV," cried Ben, becoming despondent.

"Okay, so we'll get you lots of books and games, and maybe a musical instrument," I said.

"Plus, you're going to get to help us with some chores, so you may not be as bored as you think," said Al.

"This is going to suck," says Ben.

"Yep, we'll get you some pioneer books so you can read about how exciting and fun it is to live without technology," interjected Anne, the librarian. "Also, Ben, please don't use tacky language in my presence."

"We can still build snowmen," Katie adds.

"Sap," says Ben.

"So, we need to rethink how we use resources such as space, water, light, food, and disposables. And, we need to plan for entertainment, and things to cheer us up and encourage us. I vote for some good books and some favorite food treats." Anne tactfully changes the subject.

Her redirect lead us into a discussion of gummy bears, board games, soda pop, and sports equipment. Well, you get the idea. After we brainstormed, we organized our ideas and came up with this chart. I encourage you to try this with your own family so you can determine your priorities.

Chapter 2   Life Without the Grid

Y2K Expectations

What will be different?	Response
Everyone's at Home for a While	⇒ Plan to use more food, toilet paper, & soap than usual.
Limited Access to More Supplies	⇒ Take an inventory of everything our family uses in a month, prioritize what we'll need. ⇒ Identify storage spaces in our house. Prefer dark, cool, off floor, away from walls, away from fumes. If you live in an apartment, store items on closet floors, put boards on top, then put your shoes on top of that. You can also store things under the bed. If you are a pack rat, clean out old magazines, clothes, etc. to create more storage space. Brainstorm about space usage. ⇒ Buy resource books, put in central location.
Garbage Stays Here	⇒ Minimize use of paper products. ⇒ Reduce packaging, repackage items before storing ⇒ Stock up on environmentally friendly cleaning products
Electronic Devices Won't Work	⇒ Make a list of electric devices such as clocks, toothbrushes, shavers, power drills and saws, watches - that must be replaced with a manual version. ⇒ Buy a solar battery charger and rechargeable batteries for things like flashlights. Take an inventory of every item you have in the house that uses a battery, list how many and what type, and stock accordingly. ⇒ Have board and card games and craft supplies on hand. ⇒ Buy leisure reading books for all members of the family.

After brainstorming with the family, Anne and I sat down to organize and make some lists.
At first, when Anne suggested we identify categories of general needs, and come up with specific action plans for each category, I accused her of being nit picky and overly organized. She insisted that the plans would help give us direction and focus, help us make decisions and prioritize, divide up responsibility, and enable us to keep track of our progress. As you've probably guessed, Anne was absolutely right.

We found that when we didn't use an action plan, we wasted time, money, and storage space. When we used the plans, things got accomplished more quickly and easily. We have a *General Household Action Plan* and individual plans for *Kitchen, Bathroom, First Aid, Electronics*, and *Entertainment and Games*. The *Kitchen* and *Bathroom* plans include inventory management columns on the right hand side, so you can use and replenish your supply. We recommend filling out these charts in pencil.

Even though we have chapters and plans in the book specifically for food storage, food preparation, water, light, heat, etc. - we discovered some general overall stuff that every household should consider. The action plans for this chapter include our own notations and examples, and leave lots of space for you to write in what your family needs. It may seem a little frivolous to include a section on entertainment. If you think preventing boredom won't be a problem, just unplug your TV, stereo, and radios for an evening and see what happens. We were amazed when we tried it. Our family didn't think we were addicted to television, until we tried to survive a weekend without it. It was not pretty.

Chapter 2 — Life Without the Grid

Let's think positively. I'll bet if you just take the *General Household Action Plan*, and put it on your refrigerator, the items will magically get done. The first thing you need to do before you start planning and buying is to figure out what you have in your house, what you use, what you won't need, and what you will need to replace essential items powered by electricity. We also are recommending using non-polluting soaps and cleaners. You can purchase these products from health food stores, or you can buy from a distributor like *Shaklee* or *Amway*, etc. We found that the distributors had products which were highly concentrated so you use less and store less, and that they offered better selection. These distributors also carry nutritional supplements and body care products, so we saved time by doing one stop shopping.

Speaking of nutritional supplements. Since we started preparing, we realized that one facet of society that may be temporarily disrupted during a grid failure is medical services. Anne decided to take a class on herbal remedies just in case access to a doctor is difficult. She is also working to put together an herbal first aid kit. The course is called "Be Your Own Doctor." It is a take-at-home course using workbooks and video. It is offered through The School of Natural Healing, which was founded by Dr. John Christopher in 1953. The School offers certification programs all the way up to Master Herbalist. For more information, you can call them at 1-800-372-8255. Herbal supplements for medicinal and nutritional purposes are also available from Christopher Enterprises. A free catalog is available by calling 1-800-453-1406 or by writing to: Christopher Enterprises, PO Box 777, Springville, UT 84663.

As you can imagine, Anne has become completely immersed in the natural healing philosophy. She's slowly convincing me. During the holidays I was fighting a cold and cough. She told me to mix honey, garlic, and cayenne pepper and eat it every few hours throughout the day. A funny thing happened. I did what she said, and the next day, I was feeling chipper. It is completely frightening to me that my sister may become a master healer. Oh well, stranger things have happened in my lifetime. After all, man walked on the moon.

Back to our mission, step one to get started is to conduct an inventory, decide how many months supply of each item you want, and what the approximate cost will be. Let's get busy!

Kitchen Supply Worksheet

Household Inventory	Size/Brand	On Hand	Goal #	Need #	Cost/ Each	Cost/ Total	Buy #	✓
Reusable Kitchen Supplies								
White Trash Bags								
Large Garbage Bags								
Paper Bags for Trash Save from grocery store								
Zip Lock Bags Wash and reuse								
Aluminum Foil								
Plastic Wrap								
Liquid Dish Soap Non-polluting and concentrated								
Steel Wool Pads								
Multi-purpose cleaner Non-polluting and concentrated								
Paper Towels Replace w/ rags mostly - start rag bag.								
Paper Napkins Replace w/ bandannas	Not Needed	0						
Coffee Filters	Not Needed	0						
Rubber Gloves								
Bleach								
Kitchen Supply Budget						$		

Kitchen Supply Worksheet

Household Inventory	Size/Brand	On Hand	Goal #	Need #	Cost/ Each	Cost/ Total	Buy #	✓
Kitchen Supplies								
Kitchen Supply Budget						$		

Bathroom Supply Worksheet

Household Inventory	Size/Brand	On Hand	Goal #	Need #	Cost/ Each	Cost/ Total	Buy #	✓
Bathroom Supplies								
Hand Soap Non-polluting								
Bath Soap Non-polluting								
Deodorant								
Lip Balm								
Sunscreen								
Birth Control								
Body Lotion								
Toothpaste								
Toothbrushes								
Dental Floss								
Toilet Paper (need 60 rolls/person/year)								
Feminine Hygiene								
Shaver								
Razor Blades								
Shaving Cream								
Shampoo (Non-polluting, concentrated)								
Conditioner								
Tissues (Replace w/ bandannas)								
Tweezers								
Nail Clippers								
Small Scissors								
Hairbrushes								
Combs								
Hair Holders/Bands								
Bathroom Supply Budget						$		

Bathroom Supply Worksheet

Household Inventory	Size/Brand	On Hand	Goal #	Need #	Cost/ Each	Cost/ Total	Buy #	✓
Bathroom Supplies								
Bathroom Supply Budget						$		

First Aid Kit Worksheet

Household Inventory	Size/Brand	On Hand	Goal #	Need #	Cost/ Each	Cost/ Total	Buy #	✓
First Aid Kit								
Hydrogen Peroxide								
Rubbing Alcohol								
First Aid Tape								
Gauze Pads								
Gauze Bandages								
Bandage Strips								
Ointment for cuts								
Snake-bite kit								
Thermometer								
Ace bandages								
Feminine hygiene								
Small scissors								
Latex gloves								
Eye wash kit								
Nail clippers								
Tweezers								
Sterile cotton balls								
Alcohol pads								
Saline solution								
Aloe gel for sunburn								
Over the Counter Or Herbal Reliever of:								
Cold Symptoms								
Headache								
Stomach Ache								
Hay fever/sinus								
Diarrhea								
Constipation								
Muscle Aches								
Yeast Infection								
Flashlight								
Matches								
Needles (splinter removal)								
Insect repellent								
Sunscreen								
Lip balm								
First Aid Kit Budget						$		

Note: For our first aid kit supplies, we do not use and replenish them, we keep them in a separate bag for emergency use only, then buy additional supplies for everyday use.

First Aid Kit Worksheet

Household Inventory	Size/Brand	On Hand	Goal #	Need #	Cost/ Each	Cost/ Total	Buy #	✓
First Aid Kit								
First Aid/Medical Budget						$		

Critical Electronic Devices Worksheet

Item	Location	Replacement	Source	✓
Time Pieces				
Digital Clock	Stove	Wind-Up $10-$16	Discount Store	
Wall Clock	Kitchen	None Needed		
Clock Radio	Master BR	Wind-Up Clock	Discount Store	
Clock Radio	Master BR	Solar Radio - $30	*Emergency Essentials Christian Family Resources Real Goods*	
Clock	Kids BR	Battery powered	Add AA battery to list	
Clock	Kids BR	Battery powered	Add AA battery to list	
Watches	Family	Battery powered	Buy new batteries	
Telephones				
Cordless	Kitchen	Replace w/analog phone		
Shavers				
Toothbrushes				
Can Opener				
Coffee Maker	Kitchen	French Press	*Williams Sonoma $30-$60*	
	Kitchen	Insulated Press	*Real Goods $65*	
	Kitchen	Non-electric Percolator	Camping Supply Store Discount Store	
Hand Mixer	Kitchen	Egg Beater	Grocery or Discount Store	
	Kitchen	Wire Whisk	Grocery or Discount Store	
Knife Sharpener	Kitchen	Manual Sharpener	Kitchen or Department Store	
Power Tools				
Budget	TOTAL	$		

Critical Electronic Devices Worksheet

Item	Location	Replacement	Source	✓
Budget	TOTAL	$		

Battery Inventory Worksheet

Item	Location	#	Type	Cost per Each	Cost per Total	Replaced w/rechargeable	✓
Flashlight	First aid kit	2	AA			8/1/98 by Al	
Flashlight	Car kit	1	AAA				
Flashlight	Master BR	2	AA				
Flashlight	Kitchen	2	C				
Clock	Kids BR	1	AA				
Clock	Kids BR	1	AA				
Radio	Master BR	2	AA				
Head Lamp	Garage	2	AA				
Head Lamp	Kitchen	2	AA				
Smoke alarm	Entry hall	1	9 volt				
Smoke alarm	Upstairs hall	1	9 volt				
Smoke alarm	Dining room	1	9 volt				
Solar battery charger	Need to order	1		$30.00	$30.00	Source: *Real Goods* or *Emergency Essentials*	
Budget	TOTAL				$		

Battery Inventory Worksheet

Item	Location	#	Type	Cost per Each	Cost per Total	Replaced w/rechargeable	✓
Solar battery charger	Need to order	1		$30.00	$30.00	Source: *Real Goods* or *Emergency Essentials*	
Budget	TOTAL				$		

Games and Entertainment Worksheet

Item	Pieces Complete?	Checked or Requested By	Cost of New	Buy New?	✓
Board Games					
Monopoly	Complete	Ben	N/A	N	✓
Candyland	Complete	Katie	N/A	N	✓
Clue	Need New	Nancy			
Card Games					
Art Supplies					
Blank Paper					
Crayons					
Craft Supplies					
Yarn					
Crochet Hooks					
Crochet Patterns					
Budget	$				

Games and Entertainment Worksheet

Item	Pieces Complete?	Checked or Requested By	Cost of New	Buy New?	✓
Budget	$				

General Household Action Plan

Tasks - Levels 1, 2, and 3 are the same	Person Responsible	Due Date	✓
Conduct Household Inventory			
Kitchen Supplies			
Bathroom Supplies			
First Aid and Medical Supplies			
Consult Family Physician on Above			
Electronic Devices			
Batteries Needed			
Entertainment/Games/Crafts			
Buy Supplies Using Worksheet			
Kitchen Supplies			
Bathroom Supplies			
First Aid and Medical Supplies			
Electronic Devices			
Batteries Needed			
Entertainment/Games/Crafts			

I signify that the Household Inventory Activities are complete.
Our Household Has Successfully Taken Action to Prepare for a Grid Failure or Natural Disaster

_____

Signed

_____

Date

Food Storage

Getting a Fix on Our Food Habits

When was the last time someone in your family went without a meal? I think for the Olsen's, it was probably when Grandma and Grandpa Olsen were stationed in Hawaii during World War II. For most Americans, having three meals a day is as expected as having air to breathe. Not only do we have access to food whenever we want it, we're accustomed to eating whatever we're in the mood for at that particular moment. At our house, we even cook different dinners for different people, depending on everybody's schedule and preferences. Al is a meat and potatoes guy. Anne eats mostly vegetables and rice, and some fish, but no meat. Ben tends to be a little picky about what type of vegetables he'll eat, what type of salad dressing, what shape the pasta is, etc. Unfortunately, I've catered to his whims all of his life, so he is accustomed to á la carte ordering at dinner. Katie, fortunately, will eat anything. I usually consume what is left sitting on the table after everyone else chooses.

Convenience rules in our kitchen. We minimize the mealtime hassle by eating lots of take out, fast food, and frozen and boxed meals. They save time, and everyone gets a choice. Anne shudders when she comes over and looks in our cupboards. "You're poisoning your children," she screams. "No wonder they are bouncing off the walls." "Look at these preservatives, chemicals, additives - horrid, horrid, horrid."

Chapter 3 Food Storage

It sure is easy to be a child nutritionist when you've never raised a child. Oops, I'm getting a wee bit off track. But, you get the point. We have become a mix it, nuke it, eat it, forget it, family when it comes to food consumption. The last time I made a salad that didn't come in a bag, or gave my kids a cookie baked in our oven was probably... Well, let's face it - it doesn't happen.

So, thinking about food storage is a little overwhelming for me. This afternoon, my sister, the healthy eating and planning wizardess is here to help me get started. Hopefully, we will come up with a good food plan that mixes Anne's ideas about vitamins and my ideas about ease. This will be a true balancing act.

Since the brainstorming worked so well before, Anne and I tried it again and came up with the following considerations for our food planning:

1. Good food is critical for family morale.
2. Neither of us has ever rationed food in our lives, so we will plan to order at least 20% more than we think we'll need. We should also assume that everyone in the family will be home for three meals a day for one month.
3. We need to anticipate every ingredient in case we don't have access to a grocery store.
4. We're going to need to include some goodies in our food plan - things like chips, soda pop, hard candy (OK, I'll admit, this was my item).
5. We may not have fresh vegetables, meat, cheese, milk, eggs, butter - all of which require refrigeration and frequent replenishment.
6. We will plan for three different timeframes: short term needs - 1 month, longer term 3-6 months, and more than that. We will buy for the longer term as our budget permits (our goal is to ultimately have one year of food storage), and even if we don't buy food for that long, we will do the planning.

Have It Your Way

Anne reminded me that our strategy was to modify our behavior as much as we can now, while we still have a safety net, so we decided to look at which of the things we're used to eating can be easily stored -- having some familiar foods will be comforting. At the same time, we'll start cooking with the new stuff we're buying. That will help us ease into this slowly. We also took a reality check: we are doing our food storage planning with the firm belief that we will actually be eating this stuff in an emergency situation. This means we are storing food that *realistically* we'd *want* to eat - not just all the weird dry stuff that some people like to take camping.

As we did research, we discovered we had several options about how to plan and store food for a month. One option is to go to a food preparedness company and buy pre-packaged configurations. If you want to spend less time planning for your one month food supply, we recommend you purchase the book *Food Storage 101: Where Do I Begin?*. The book is the most comprehensive, easy-to-use tool we've found for planning and implementing a short or long term food supply. It is available from Peggy Layton by calling (435) 835-0311 or by visiting her web site at www.ut-biz.com/homestoragecookin/. You can write to Peggy at PO Box 44, Manti, Utah, 84642 for a product brochure.

Another alternative is to purchased pre-packaged food supplies that will feed your family from one month up to one or two years from a preparedness food company. The advantage to this approach is that you don't need to spend much time. Just get on the Web or make a phone call, and they ship the stuff to you. The disadvantages are many. Ordering food this way may be more expensive. Also, you will be trusting averages for the quantities of food and serving sizes you have, and you probably won't be eating the foods you like best. Another hazard of this approach

Chapter 3   Food Storage

is that it is easier to stash the food cases in a corner of the basement, and not open them until an emergency occurs. This can be dangerous. In the first place, your family members may be allergic to certain foods or ingredients, or may be unwilling to eat what is provided. In the second place, no one wants to be experimenting with unfamiliar food and new preparation methods under the stress of an emergency.

When building a one month supply, we advocate buying some basic foods from the preparedness companies, then planning menus and buying whatever else you need from your grocery store, food co-op, or membership warehouse. Planning menus will ensure that you eat what you are accustomed to, and that you have adequate amounts of various menu items.

We started with the basics most people need to cook with - butter, cheese, eggs, milk, etc. It turns out that you can buy powdered butter, powdered margarine, powdered eggs, powdered milk (much better than the stuff we drank when we were kids - blah!), powdered shortening, and cheese powder - all from companies that specialize in providing food for long term storage and emergencies. Simply add water to the powder, and *voilà*, you have a great alternative to the fresh items you would normally buy. These powdered miracles can be purchased from preparedness food companies. If you are trying to locate a store near you who sells preparedness supplies, look for bread baking supply stores and alternative energy product suppliers. The millennium bug has motivated some of these stores to carry new products.

Most foods from preparedness companies are packaged in number 10 cans or 5 gallon buckets. (A number 10 can is about as big as a one gallon can of paint. If you've ever noticed construction people or painters carrying around those big white plastic buckets with tight fitting lids, then you've seen a 5 gallon bucket. They weigh about 30 pounds when filled with food.) If you're planning a one month food supply, you might buy a few things in # 10 cans. For longer term storage, 5 gallon buckets will be more practical for dry goods like flour, pasta, and beans.

We're now going to demonstrate how we planned for Level 1 - for one month without access to a grocery store. Every single family in the United States should do this. The first step is to order the following items from a preparedness food company:

Level 1 Basics for Family of Four

Item	Packaging	Amount	Quantity Needed	Approx Cost/Ea.	Total Cost	✓
Powdered Milk	# 10 Can	1.5 cans/person/mo*	6	$14.00	$64.00	
Powdered Butter	# 10 Can	176 1 Tbl. servings	2	$23.00	$46.00	
Powdered Eggs	# 10 Can	108 (1 egg) servings	1	$20.00	$20.00	
Cheese Powder	# 10 Can	130 1/8 c servings	1	$18.00	$18.00	
Total for family of 4					$148.00	

Note: For single person, order 2 cans of milk, and 1 can of other items, for a total of $89.00.
*Each #10 can of milk makes approximately 20 quarts when mixed with water.

We discovered a few things about buying preparedness foods. Most of the retailers of bulk food obtain their food from the same single source (except for a few organic and natural food providers we'll discuss later), so you should compare prices for the basics suggested above. Chances are, you are buying the same product, only with a different label. Also, the good thing about buying from these companies is that the food is packaged for long term (10 or more years) storage.

When we do our 3-6 month and longer plans, we will increase the amount of food from these sources. Also, keep in mind that preparedness food companies often give a discount on

Chapter 3 — Food Storage

essentials like powdered milk if you purchase a whole case. Compare prices, and save money by buying cases when you can. A few words to the wise: Another way to save money is to order now. As awareness of the millennium bug becomes more prevalent, demand for most of the items in this book will go up. As the available supply decreases, prices will definitely increase. We've also noticed recently that lead times to acquire these foods are increasing. This is another good reason to purchase these items as soon as you can.

Now, let's talk about the things we need to eat every day to be healthy. As we did research, we discovered that planning for food storage can get complicated. After we looked at the USDA Food Group Pyramid, and some books on food storage, we realized that planning nutritionally balanced meals by computing serving sizes involved more than we want to take on for one month of storage. At this point, our main priority is having enough food in the house so we can serve three meals a day. Therefore, we decided to design menus for seven days and try to incorporate a healthy mix of ingredients from all of the necessary food groups - grains, vegetables, fruits, protein, and fats/oils. As we extend the length of our food supply, we can become more scientific in calculating nutritional value. For now, we'll stock up on a supply of multivitamins and take them every day.

We found it easiest to plan meals for one week, and then quadruple everything. We tried to reduce our meat consumption as much as possible. Here are examples of Menu Planning Charts. I planned days 1 through 4, Anne planned days 5 through 7. You could also plan menus for two weeks, then double everything.

Menu Planner

Menu Day One	Menu Day Two	Menu Day Three	Menu Day Four
Breakfast	**Breakfast**	**Breakfast**	**Breakfast**
Cold Cereal	Pancakes	Cheese Omelets	Corned Beef Hash
Milk	Syrup or Honey	Hash Browns	Scrambled Eggs
Biscuits	Butter	Salsa	Biscuits
Peaches	Apple Sauce	Corn Muffins	Milk
Hot Chocolate	Milk	Milk	Coffee
Coffee	Coffee	Coffee	
Lunch	**Lunch**	**Lunch**	**Lunch**
Flour Tortillas	Italian Veg Soup	Broccoli/Rice Soup	Macaroni & Cheese
Refried Beans	Saltines	Bread and Butter	Green Beans
Salsa	Peanut Butter	Fruit Cocktail	Pears
Canned Corn	Milk	Milk	Milk
Milk	Cookies	Cookies	Hard Candy
Small Candy Bars			
Dinner	**Dinner**	**Dinner**	**Dinner**
Spaghetti	Tuna Casserole	Beef Stew	Chicken a la King
Meat Sauce	Green Beans	Spinach	Peas and Carrots
Green Beans	Pears	Mashed Potatoes	Bread and Butter
Garlic Bread	Bread and Butter	Bread and Butter	Applesauce
Milk	Milk	Milk	Milk
Herbal Tea	Herbal Tea	Herbal Tea	Herbal Tea
Brownies			
Snacks	**Snacks**	**Snacks**	**Snacks**
Popcorn	Sunflower Seeds	Pretzels	Snack Crackers
Dried Fruit	Fruit Roll Ups	Granola Bars	Soda Pop
Bags of Juice	Grapefruit Juice	Grape Juice	Juice Boxes
Pet Food	**Pet Food**	**Pet Food**	**Pet Food**

Menu Planner

Menu Day Five	Menu Day Six	Menu Day Seven	
Breakfast	**Breakfast**	**Breakfast**	
Oatmeal	Bean Burritos w/Green Chile	Protein Shakes with Powdered Milk	
Honey	Hash Browns	Blueberry Muffins	
Butter	Milk	Milk	
Raisins	Coffee	Cranberry Juice	
Milk		Coffee	
Coffee			
Lunch	**Lunch**	**Lunch**	
Black Bean Soup	Garden Veg Soup	Potato Soup	
Corn Muffins	Peanut Butter Sandwiches	Oatmeal Muffins	
Milk	Milk	Milk	
Graham Crackers	Oatmeal Cookies	Vanilla Wafers	
Dinner	**Dinner**	**Dinner**	
Chicken Curry	Cream of Shrimp Soup over Couscous	Salmon Loaf	
Red Lentil Dal	Muffins	Bean Salad	
White Rice	Butter	Bread and Butter	
Naan (Indian bread)	Spinach	Corn	
Milk	Milk	Milk	
Herbal Tea	Herbal Tea	Herbal Tea	
Apple Pie	Hard Candy	Chocolate Cupcakes	
Snacks	**Snacks**	**Snacks**	
Pretzels	Pretzels	Mixed Nuts	
Rice Krispie Treats	Dried Fruit	Goldfish	
Apple Juice	Cranberry Juice	Apple Juice	
Pet Food	**Pet Food**	**Pet Food**	**Pet Food**

Chapter 3 — Food Storage

Then we tallied the items and ingredients in our menus. We assumed 4 adult servings meal to give a little extra, then added approximately 20% more to our purchase quantity. Only you know how much people in your family eat. Does a standard sized can of spinach equal four servings for your family, or two? You will need to decide. When in doubt, we added a little more. We know we'll eventually use whatever food we buy. Items purchased at the grocery store can generally be used safely for one to two years. Canned goods have an expiration date on them. Pasta and dried beans last even longer. This is a sample of how to prepare your own planning chart. The packaging type will impact the quantities you need.

Meal Items	# Meals Served At	# Svg/ Meal	Total Svg	Package Type	Servings Per Package	Qty to Buy	✓
Baking and Bread							
Biscuits (Bisquick)	8	6	48			1 box	
Blueberry Muffins	4	6	24			4 boxes	
Corn Muffins	8	6	48	Box	8	8 boxes	
Flour	24	4	76			20 lbs	
Flour Tortillas	2	6	12	Bag	12	2 bags	
Yeast for Bread	24	4	76			56 packets	
Breakfast Needs							
Cheese Omelet Eggs	4	6	24	# 10 can	108	In Basics	
Cold Cereal	4	4	16	13.5 oz	7	4 boxes	
Hash Browns	8	6	48	Foil pouch	4	12 pouches	
Oatmeal	12	6	72			6 boxes	
Pancakes (Bisquick)	4	6	48			1 box	
Scrambled Eggs	4	6	24	# 10 can		In Basics	
Beverages							
Apple, Cranberry, Grapefruit Juices	16	6	96	Jug		4 Jugs	
Coffee	31	4	124			5 lbs	
Herbal Tea	31	2	62			8 boxes	
Hot Chocolate	12	6	72				
Juice Mixes						4 cases	
Milk	93	4		# 10 cans		In Basics	
Soda Pop						8 cases	
Fruit							
Apple Sauce	8	6	48	Jars		6 jars	
Dried Fruit						6 bags	
Fruit Cocktail	8	4	24			8 cans	
Peaches - Canned	8	4	24			8 cans	
Pears - Canned	8	4	24			8 cans	

Level 1 Shopping Planner

Meal Items	# Meals Served At	# Svg/ Meal	Total Svg	Package Type	Servings Per Package	Qty to Buy	✓
Main Ingredients							
Bread Crumbs						1 box	
Butter	93	4	372			In Basics	
Cheese Powder	4	6	24	# 10 can	130	In Basics	
Honey	8	4	32			2 Jars	
Onion Flakes						1 Jar	
Peanut Butter	8	4	32			4 large jars	
Protein Powder	8	6	48	Cans		2 large cans	
Soup - Canned	20	6	120		2	60 cans	
Syrup	4	6	24			2 bottles	
White Rice	8	6	48			10 pounds	
Meat & Main Dishes							
Beef Stew	4	6	48			8 Large Cans	
Chicken á la king	4	8	32			8 large Cans	
Chicken - Canned	8	6	48			16 sm cans	
Corned Beef Hash	4	4	16			4 large cans	
Salmon - Canned	4	6	24			8 sm cans	
Tuna - Canned	4	8	32			6 large cans	
Soup and Lunch							
Assorted Soup	20	6	120			40 cans	
Cream Mush Soup	4	8	32			6 cans	
Crm of Shrimp Soup	8	6	48			16 cans	
Macaroni & Cheese	4	6	24			12 boxes	
Pasta & Sauces							
Couscous	8	6	48			8 boxes	
Meat Sauce In Jar	4	6	24			4 Jars	
Noodles (Tuna Cass)	4	8	32			4 bags	
Spaghetti Noodles	4	6	24			4 lbs	

Level 1 Shopping Planner

Meal Items	# Meals Served At	# Svg/ Meal	Total Svg	Package Type	Servings Per Package	Qty to Buy	✓
Snacks							
Candy Bars - Small						6 bags	
Cookies	12	8	76			8 dozen	
Fruit Roll Ups						6 boxes	
Graham Crackers						4 boxes	
Hard Candy						6 bags	
Popcorn						6 jars	
Pretzels						4 bags	
Saltines	4	4	16			1 box	
Snack Crackers						6 boxes	
Desserts							
Apple Pie	4	4	16			16 indiv.	
Chocolate Cupcakes	4	4	16			2 dozen	
Rice Krispie Treats						4 boxes	
Goldfish						2 pounds	
Mixed Nuts						2 pounds	
Vegetables							
Bean Salad	8	4	32			8 cans/jars	
Corn - Canned	8	4	24		4	4 large cans	
Green Beans	8	6	48			16 cans	
Peas and Carrots	4	4	16			8 sm. cans	
Red Lentils	8	6	48			2 pounds	
Refried Beans	8	6	48			8 large cans	
Salsa	8	6	48			3 Jars	
Spinach - Canned	16	4	64			16 cans	

Chapter 3   Food Storage

You probably noticed that our one month planning assumed using only canned meats and vegetables or boxed items such as cereal, muffins, pancake mix, and macaroni and cheese. For simplicity, we also assumed the only thing we would bake is bread, biscuits, and muffins. The cookies, cupcakes, apple pies, etc., are commercial products that contain preservatives - the kind of individually wrapped desserts we pack in our kids' school lunches today. Tortillas can be stored up to one month, as long they are in a cool place. After that, they'll need to be made from scratch. We bought basics (powdered eggs, milk, butter) from the food storage companies, and then bulk items such as rice, pancake mix, hot chocolate, juice, etc. from the membership warehouse, and everything else at the grocery store. We also took an inventory of items like flour, oil, shortening, honey, cornstarch, cornmeal, yeast, shortening, vinegar, and spices. We bought extras and put them in a special storage cupboard.

To get an estimated budget, we went to a regular grocery store and priced everything. The total grocery bill for our one month food supply came to $939.41. You can save lots of money by comparing bulk prices at the various preparedness companies, or by buying from a membership warehouse or food co-op. You can also spend less by gardening and canning.

If you decide to buy in bulk from anywhere, you need to consider a few things. Leftovers from # 10 cans can be placed in canning jars, and vacuum sealed with a manual pump and pump tabs. This tool removes the air from the jar, allowing you to store longer without refrigeration. The tool is called a Pump-n-Seal, and costs approximately $20. You can buy it from most preparedness food companies (see Sources at end of chapter). Items like rice, flour, etc. purchased in sacks should be stored for the long term in food grade, 5 gallon buckets with food grade plastic bag liners. These can also be purchased from the sources listed.

To add fresh foods to the above, consider that potatoes, onions, carrots, and hard squashes (butternut, acorn), will store well in a cool, dry place (such as a basement) for at least a month. Green tomatoes wrapped in newspaper and stored in a basement will ripen. Also, you can grow sprouts and lettuce indoors. We'll talk more about this when we talk about gardening and Level 3 preparation.

Your own list of a full month's supply probably will look a little overwhelming. Keep in mind what your monthly grocery bill is today, what you spend eating meals out, and what you spend at the school cafeteria and for miscellaneous snacks, what you spend on coffee on the run, and for snacks at the vending machines at work. Once you add all of those extras, you'll realize you will pay the same amount or maybe even less than the average month's bill for what you will be storing.

Chapter 3 — Food Storage

Do's and Don'ts

Before we talk about storing food for more than a month, we thought we'd discuss how and where to store food. Here are some general guidelines:

DO

1. Store food in a place that is as cool, dark, and dry.
2. Place containers on shelves, wood palates, or boards.
3. Store food at least six inches away from a wall.
4. Label each container with the purchase date and contents.
5. Store food in more than one location if possible.
6. Restock by placing newest items toward the back, use older items first.
7. Store food only in food grade containers.

DON'T

1. Store food in an attic (too hot) or a garage (toxic exhaust fumes can penetrate plastic food containers and contaminate food).
2. Store food in trash bags or non-food grade trash cans. They have been treated with pesticides.
3. Place containers on the floor. They can mold or mildew or be invaded by rodents or insects.
4. Store food touching a wall. Mold or mildew can form on the containers.

If you live in a house with a basement; the basement is the best place to store food. Al built us some simple shelves under our stairs, and away from the window. This is great because it gives us two sided access to our food, and makes it much easier to see what we have and replenish our stock.

If you have a garage, you can move some items that you would normally store inside like your vacuum cleaner, sports equipment, and out of season shoes and clothing (we put them in big suitcases we rarely use) - put those items in the garage, and store food inside your house.

For those people who live in apartments or dwellings without basements or garages, have fun and be creative. We have one friend who put plywood on her closet floor, placed her food storage cans on top of the plywood, then put another layer of plywood, and her shoes on top. Another friend converted her linen closet to a food storage pantry, and put her sheets and towels on the top shelf of her clothes closet. You can also store food under your bed on plywood. To make space in your kitchen, you can pack infrequently used items, like Grandma's china, in boxes (they can be stored anywhere), then use the freed up space for food storage. If you must, you can put your storage items in a big cardboard box, throw a tablecloth over it, slam a lamp on top, and you've got a new table plus food storage. You can also replace your coffee table with a footlocker or trunk and put food inside. One word of advice to pack rats short on storage space. If you can't eat it, wear it, drink it, or use it for heating or cooking - consider getting rid of it.

Chapter 3   Food Storage

In *Chapter 2*, we talked about storing extra cleaning supplies. If you storage space is at a premium in your house, obviously finding space for food, water, and first aid supplies will be the number one priority.

Now it's time to do your own one month planning. We were able to complete our planning and shopping list in a single Saturday morning. Then, we took some money out of our savings account, and went shopping at the grocery store and membership warehouse the next Saturday. We stocked our shelves on Sunday afternoon, and were finished with our Level 1 Food Storage activity in only two weekends. The sense of accomplishment and security we achieved were well worth the investment. You will be surprised at how relieved you'll feel after accomplishing these tasks.

Step One is to fill out menus for seven days. Use the blank worksheets on the following pages.

Level 1 Food Storage Menu

Menu	Menu	Menu	Menu
Breakfast	**Breakfast**	**Breakfast**	**Breakfast**
Cold cereal	Cold cereal	Cold cereal	Cereal
milk	milk	milk	milk
Lunch	**Lunch**	**Lunch**	**Lunch**
PB&J	Grilled cheese	Beef stew	Mac & cheese
Pears	Mand oranges	Fruit cocktail	Green beans
			Pears
			Cookies
Dinner	**Dinner**	**Dinner**	**Dinner**
Vege soup/bu__	Spaghetti	Tuna casserole	Chick noodle soup
	Peas	Green beans	
Snacks	**Snacks**	**Snacks**	**Snacks**
Popcorn			
Pretzels			

Level 1 Food Storage Menus

Menu	Menu	Menu	Menu
Breakfast	**Breakfast**	**Breakfast**	**Breakfast**
Cereal	Cereal	Cereal	
Lunch	**Lunch**	**Lunch**	**Lunch**
Bean soup	PB&J	Grilled cheese	
Dinner	**Dinner**	**Dinner**	**Dinner**
Chili	Clam chowder	Salmon	
	Bisquets		
	Honey		
Snacks	**Snacks**	**Snacks**	**Snacks**

Now, take your menu items and convert them to a list for shopping. Use the worksheets below.

Level 1 Shopping List

Meal Items	# Meals Served At	# Svg/ Meal	Total Svg	Package Type	Servings Per Package	Qty to Buy	✓

Level 1 Shopping List

Meal Items	# Meals Served At	# Svg/ Meal	Total Svg	Package Type	Servings Per Package	Qty to Buy	✓

Level 1 Shopping List

Meal Items	# Meals Served At	# Svg/ Meal	Total Svg	Package Type	Servings Per Package	Qty to Buy	✓

Level 1 Shopping List

Meal Items	# Meals Served At	# Svg/ Meal	Total Svg	Package Type	Servings Per Package	Qty to Buy	✓

Sources for Preparedness Food

Company	Telephone	Web Site	Address
The Country Store Preparedness Center	(888) 311-8940	www.healthyharvest.com	11013 A NE 39th St. Vancouver, WA 98662
Christian Family Resources	(719) 962-3228 Monday-Friday 1-5 p.m. MST (Orders Only)	N/A Send $2 for Catalog to PO Box	PO Box 405 Kit Carson, CO 80825
Emergency Essentials	(800) 999-1863	www.beprepared.com	165 S. Mtn. Way Dr. Orem, UT 84058
Food For Thought of Montana	(888) 635-8925	www.e-foodforthought.com	334 Orchard Ridge Rd. Kalispell, MT 59901
Forever Foods	(800) 851-2634	www.foreverfoods.com	325 E. Washington St. #137 Sequim, WA 98382
H&W Distributors	(888) 301-8307	www.zianet.com/hwd	316 E. Hall St., Box 859 Hatch, NM 87937
High Country Gourmet	(801) 426-4383	N/A	225 S. Mtn. Way Dr. Orem, UT 84058
Happy Hovel Storable Foods	(800) 637-7772	www.wwmagic.com	PO Box 781 Yelm, WA 98597
Lakeridge Food Storage	(800) 336-7127	www.shopsite.com/lfs	896 E. 640 N. Orem, UT 84097
Mountain Magic	(800) 979-2665	www.mtn-magic.com	12371 W. 64th Ave. Arvada, CO 80004
Millennium Gourmet Food Reserves	(800) 500-9893	Email food@itsnet.com	PO Box 50597 Provo, UT 84605
Noah's Pantry	(888) Y2K-NOAH	www.noahspantry.com	PO Box 1441 Claremore, OK 74018
Ready Made Resources	(800) 627-3809	www.cococo.net/rmr	239 Cagle Road Tellico Plains, TN 37385
Survival Products	(215) 722-7797	N/A	7975 Oxford Avenue Philadelphia, PA 19111

Disclaimer: *This list was compiled for your convenience. It does not guarantee the availability or quality of products or suppliers, nor is it a complete list of potential suppliers. As information changes over time, this list may not be accurate. Conduct your own research before purchasing products.*

Note: Most of these companies also sell water storage and purification supplies. If you want to save money on shipping, you can refer to *Chapter 4* on *Water Basics*, and place a single order for Food Storage Basics and Water Supplies at the same time.

Level 1 Food Storage Action Plan

Tasks	Person Responsible	Due Date	✓
Order Food Basics from Preparedness Company			
Powdered Milk			
Powdered Eggs			
Powdered Butter			
Cheese Powder			
Plan Menus for at Least One Week			
Breakfast			
Lunch			
Dinner			
Snacks			
List Ingredients and Quantities for Shopping			
Identify/Create Storage Spaces			
Buy All Items on List			
Date and Label Each Item as it is Stored			
Begin Cooking with Stored Food			

*I signify that the Food Storage Action Plan Activities for Level 1 are complete.
Our Household Has Taken the Crucial First Step to Prepare for a Grid Failure or Natural Disaster*

_____

Signed

_____

Date

Chapter 3   Food Storage

Level 2 Food Storage Preparedness

Three to Six Months of Food Storage plus Nutritional Supplements

Entire books have been written on the subject of food storage. The purpose of this book is to encourage everyone, who is able, to prepare at Level 1, and store a one month food supply for each member of the household.

For Level 2 preparation, we suggest storing food for three to six months, and adding nutritional supplements and sprouts to your food storage program. Most of the preparedness food companies sell the same type of food you would buy in the grocery store, only packaged for longer term storage and freshness. One thing you can do to add fresh food to your food storage program is to sprout beans and grains. You can purchase sprouting trays from many of the companies where you buy beans and wheat in bulk. Depending on how they are processed, some grains may not be suitable for sprouting. If you intend to sprout a certain bean or grain, doublecheck with the supplier before you buy them.

Sprouts provide vitamins, proteins, minerals, live enzymes, and fiber. Live enzymes aid in digestion and convert starches into sugars, protein into amino acids, and fats into fatty acids. Sprouts are also a source of antioxidants. It only takes two to four days to grow sprouts.

Entire books have been written on nutritional supplements. We are not experts in this area. Also, individual needs and expert's opinions vary. You may want to investigate what nutritional supplements are best for you by visiting a health food store or by consulting with your physician. The four things you should consider having in your nutritional supplement supply are a good multi-vitamin, mineral supplements such as calcium and magnesium, antioxidants, and digestive enzymes. Once you decide what is appropriate, nutritional supplements can be ordered from many sources.

An excellent reference book for your Y2K library is *Making the Best of Basics* by James Talmage Stevens. The book has extremely detailed information on planning for long term storage and extensive reference lists on where to buy essential items. It is available at *Amazon.com* or from preparedness stores.

Planning for a 3-6 month food supply will mainly involve buying a few more items in bulk - either in #10 cans or buckets, or buying larger cans or cases of food from a merchandise warehouse. You will want to increase your supply of powdered milk (less expensive if purchased in cases of 12 cans), and add several more cans of powdered butter, cheese, and eggs. You can also add dehydrated hash browns and mashed potatoes from a preparedness company to your storage.

We were lucky to find out about a grain sale at our local preparedness store, and stocked up on 45 pound buckets of things like pinto beans, navy beans, basmati rice, black beans, lentils, couscous, popcorn, wheat, seven grain mix, spelt, and oat groats. I've been amazed at how using items from food storage has decreased our grocery bill. I put a device called a Gamma Seal lid (available from our food supplier) on the buckets I use the most, so I can simply unscrew the lids when I need to access the food. This gives me incentive to use the bulk foods and learn to cook with them, and enables me to color code my buckets. We also put labels with dates on all of our buckets and cans so we know when we bought them. To tell the truth, I've never slept better than I do now knowing that we have an adequate food supply for our family. Buying food this way has become a new way of life for the Olsens.

Chapter 3 — Food Storage

Purchasing in bulk also provides an excellent opportunity to work with your neighbors, friends, and/or family members who are also putting together food storage. Everyone can save money if the group buys items on sale and in large quantities, and divides them between several families. If you live in an urban environment, you may want to work with your tenant association or the other people in your building, buy in bulk, and rent a shared storage space.

An easy way to slowly increase from a one month food storage supply is to buy two of every non-perishable item your family regularly eats every time you go to the grocery store. Use one, and store the other. Keep in mind that most of the food you buy from a grocery store or membership warehouse will only have a one or two year shelf life. We take advantage of the weekly "buy one and get one free" specials offered by local grocery stores. You'll be amazed at how quickly your storage space will diminish and your food supply will grow when you begin implementing a few small changes into your food buying habits.

Chapter 3   Food Storage

Level 3 Food Storage Preparedness

One or More Years of Food Storage plus Gardening and Grinding Grains

Level 3 preparation will involve planning for and storing food for one year or more. Planning to store food for more than six months is a little more complicated because the shelf life of each food now must be considered. One way to reduce the amount of food you need to store, and to have a more nutritious and appealing diet is to grow and preserve some of your own food.

If you have never raised a vegetable garden before, now is an excellent time to start. An interesting book on organic, biointensive gardening (a method successfully used in the US and third world countries that requires less space and less water) is John Jeavons' *How to Grow More Vegetables*. The book, along with a myriad of information on organic gardening, is available through *Ecology Action*, 5798 Ridgewood Road, Willits, CA 95490, Telephone: (707) 459-0150. Since soil types and climates vary greatly, you should also visit your local bookstore to find reference books on gardening in your specific part of the country. Universities in your area should also have an agricultural extension service to help you determine which fruits and vegetables thrive at your altitude and climate.

Whenever possible, use non-hybrid seeds in your garden. A vegetable grown from a non-hybrid seed will produce seeds that can be planted and will yield vegetables the next year, enabling you to grow and save your own seeds. Most of us are accustomed to planting hybrid seeds. Because these seeds have been genetically mutated, they are not able to regenerate, so must be replenished every year.

If you want to preserve your food, you need to consider canning, dehydrating, and root cellaring. Root cellaring can be done in an ordinary basement. Certain vegetables such as potatoes, onions, carrots, and garlic can be kept without spoiling for months when properly prepared and maintained in storage. Canning vegetables can be complicated and requires special equipment. Canning and storage methods and tools will be discussed in Chapter 5 on food preparation.

An excellent way to share resources and to help your neighbors prepare would be to organize a community garden near your home. Many families can participate in preparing the ground, planting, watering, weeding, harvesting, and canning the output. This is an approach that can save money and help everyone learn new skills.

If you intend to store more than a one year supply of food, grinding your own grains and seeds for flour, cereal, and snacks is suggested. Whole grains store much longer than flour and cereal (which have a shelf life of six to twelve months), and more of their nutritional value is retained when they are stored whole, then ground as needed. Wheat can be stored indefinitely, if packaged to prevent insect and rodent infestation. Barley, corn, and oats can be stored and usable for up to five years. Whole beans have a shelf life of two to three years. *Happy Hovel Foods* in Yelm, Washington has a wonderful catalog that can help you decide which grains to order and what quantity you need for your family. To order, call 1-800-637-7772. Grinding grains is explored further in *Chapter 5*.

Water Basics

Growing up in Colorado, we can remember times when our town closed down for a few days because of a major snow storm, and we weren't able to get to the grocery store. Most of the people we know store extra food in the winter - just in case. Even though we've had some significant storms and occasionally lost power or our telephone service, I can't remember a time when I turned on the faucet and water didn't flow out.

My grandmother was born in the late 1800's. She lived much of her life without electricity, running water, or telephones. When Anne and I were little kids, we used to go up to the Colorado mountains with my grandparents to a cabin that Grandpa had built. As we got older, electricity and an indoor bathroom were added. But, in the beginning, water came out of a hand pump in the kitchen sink, Grandma cooked on a wood stove, we took baths in a washtub, and we drank water out of a ladle from a white enamel canister. To our grandmother, summer weekends at the cabin were probably more enjoyable than being in her house in the city with modern conveniences. When we were kids, staying at the cabin was our favorite adventure. As an adult, the thought of living without running water for more than a day or so is a little bit disheartening to me.

Do you realize that the average American uses between 100 and 150 gallons of water every day? And that water weighs approximately 8 pounds per gallon? In one month, our family of four, with our typical wasteful usage today, probably uses 12,000-15,000 gallons of water. In an emergency, the amount of water most people can get by with is one gallon per day. For a family of four, the absolute minimum one month's supply would be 120 gallons. That allows half a gallon for drinking, and half a gallon for cooking and washing.

Chapter 4   Water Basics

When the temperature outside is hot, or when physical exertion is increased, water consumption increases.

The main reason to store water is because it is the most critical ingredient needed to sustain life. While a human being can survive for several weeks without food, the probability of existing for more than a few days without water is very low. When planning for a grid failure, which is more important - storing water or storing food? We've had an ongoing debate at the Olsen house about what might happen if water and food distribution systems are impacted by the millennium bug or by a natural disaster. I argue that water trucks would probably come to our neighborhoods, and whatever water was provided would be acceptable for our family. Plus, we can haul water from sources near our house, such as irrigation ditches. I would much rather have food in the house, so we can eat what we want, instead of relying on what might be provided in an emergency. Al, on the other hand, argues that we shouldn't depend on outside sources, if possible, for anything but emergency medical care. He thinks we should store as much water as we'll need for a month.

We've finally reached a compromise. We'll store large quantities of both food and water, and cut our entertainment budget even further to pay for it. Al and I also disagree about preparing our house in case of a water distribution failure. Al thinks we should turn off the water in December of 1999, and have a plumber blow air through our pipes. That way, if the water supply is disrupted, our pipes won't freeze before the situation is resolved. He also suggests we plug our drains with rags and duct tape in case the public sewer system backs up. This implies we begin using an outhouse in December, also. The idea of intentionally ceasing to use indoor plumbing seems a little extreme to me. But, if our pipes froze or the sewer backed up into our house, we would have an incredible mess, especially if we had limited access to clean water. We will wait to see how things develop, and keep a close eye on the progress of our public utility company. A lesson for your family is - don't expect to agree on every issue surrounding a grid failure - even within your own household.

Water Storage

If our family was without running water, we would want to be sure to have at least a one month supply of clean drinking water stored in our house. That means storing at least 30 gallons of water per person. You can store more if you have room. Keep in mind that pets will also require water. Like food, water should be stored in a plastic food grade container, on a wood pallet off of the floor, in a cool, dark area. Food grade plastic water containers are available in 5, 15, 30, and 55 gallon sizes, and can be obtained from the same sources we discussed in Chapter 3 that sell preparedness food. Larger water storage containers and towers are available from *Jade Mountain* in Boulder, Colorado. (See mail order resource table at end of chapter.)

Used storage drums may be used, and can be purchased from beverage companies. Be aware that plastic containers retain the taste of whatever has been stored in them before. So, if you buy used containers, you will risk compromising the flavor of the water. Water does not store well in metal containers. They can rust and/or cause the water to have an unpleasant taste.

New 55 gallon plastic storage containers sell for about $60. They are approximately the same size as those big garbage cans that most of us in suburbia take to the curb on trash day. A special wrench and spigot are required to open the container and remove water. The water storage containers obtained from preparedness companies have been designed for durability, and to withstand hot and cold temperatures, so they can be stored outdoors. They can also be used to collect rain water, or to melt snow in to help increase your water supply. If you have the storage space, you can store water in the larger containers. If not, you can use 5 gallon drums which can

Chapter 4 — Water Basics

be easily moved and stacked. Obviously, a limited supply of food grade water storage containers are available. After reading this, take action and begin storing water immediately.

If you don't have the space or can't afford storage containers, you can store water in plastic 2 liter containers that soda pop comes in. Used milk jugs aren't as good, because they are biodegradable and will self-destruct in about six months. They also contain milk residue which will seep into your water, no matter how well you wash them. For shorter term water storage, you can use 1 gallon or 2 1/2 gallon plastic bottles which originally contained water, but they must be stored in a protected area inside your house to prevent breakage. Bleach containers should not be used. Glass containers such as apple juice jugs are also usable, but they can break, and the metal lids on them are susceptible to rust.

Whatever container you use, clean it with a solution of 1/8 teaspoon of chlorine bleach mixed with a gallon of hot water. Cleaning the container with bleach instead of dish washing detergent will ensure that your water does not contain soap residue. A small amount of bleach residue will not harm you. After cleaning with the water and bleach solution, rinse the container thoroughly with plain water and place it in it's storage location (a 55 gallon drum weighs 440 pounds and will not be movable when filled), on a wooden pallet or on boards. Fill the container with water from the source you normally drink from, seal the lid with a spigot wrench, and label the container with the date.

Most of the time, the water will not need to be treated for storage. Some preparedness companies recommend adding purification agents to stored water. Depending on the purity of your drinking water, you can consider adding purification tablets, Aerobic Oxygen, or food grade hydrogen peroxide to your water. These are available from the same sources as water barrels. Opinions vary on whether or not chlorine bleach should be used to purify drinking water. If you store water from the source you drink from today, and if you replace the water once a year, most sources agree that the water will be acceptable for drinking. If you drink from your stored water supply, and it tastes flat, you can reincorporate oxygen and improve the taste by simply transferring the water back and forth between two containers.

Ideally, water should be stored in a dry, cool, dark area on a wood pallet or on boards, off of the floor and at least 12 inches from a wall. Water not be stored in the garage because of auto fumes, and should not be near paint, chemicals, or any other toxic substance. The reason for this is that plastic is permeable, which means that fumes can penetrate the containers and contaminate the contents.

Sources of Water

In an emergency, reducing your family's water usage to 1% of what you normally use will be challenging. Ideally, if you store one gallon of water per person per day for one month, you would prefer to use that water for drinking only. Finding other sources of water will be crucial. Entire books have been written about obtaining and purifying water. We will share some of our basic findings here, and encourage you to do your own research if you have the time.

Supplementing your usable water supply will involve locating, transporting, purifying, and storing water. To locate water, keep in mind that water only comes from two sources, the sky or the ground. The easiest way to increase your water supply is through rain water retention. You can order devices for your house to filter rain water through your roof gutters, and attach special hose devices to your drain spouts that will allow you to direct rain water into a holding receptacle. United Airlines *High Street Emporium* catalog sells rain gutter pumps for approximately $8 each which block leaves and debris and siphon rainwater down the spout. They also offer a flexible

Chapter 4 — Water Basics

hose that extends your downspout of approximately $15 each. This can be used to divert water to a holding receptacle. Some home improvement stores sell these devices, as well.

Potential types of holding tanks include: 55 gallon water drums, a galvanized steel bin or trough, or an in-ground storage place. If you have a very large yard, you can dig a big hole and line it with bricks or a tarp. Keep in mind, that in an emergency, this land space may be needed for other uses such garbage and waste disposal. We prefer to place a trough like the ones used to water livestock next to the house and cover it with a tarp after it rains to protect the water from leaves, dirt, and evaporation. Troughs are available from feed stores. Inflatable wading pools can also be used for water retention, but need to be checked regularly for leaks. Be sure to have a patch kit and air pump on hand if you choose this method. If you live in the city, this is an excellent option for obtaining water. Take the uninflated pool to the roof of your building, inflate it, and use it to collect rainwater.

Another potential source of water after an emergency is to haul it from water trucks that might come to your neighborhood, or from lakes, streams, or irrigation ditches. Since a single gallon of water weighs eight pounds, water should be transported in 5 gallon containers. These are available from emergency preparedness, camping, or mountaineering stores, and are inexpensive (approximately $5 each). The containers can be moved using a wheelbarrow, child's toy wagon, or hand truck. Take a walk around your neighborhood now and locate potential natural water sources.

If you live in a multi-level building, you will need to be prepared to haul water up stairs. You may want to obtain a water container that collapses (available in mountaineering stores), and purchase a backpack that it will fit in when it is full of water. Since 5 gallons of water weighs 40 pounds, it will be difficult to carry this amount of water with your hands.

Sources of water within your home include hot water heaters, toilet tanks (not bowls), swimming pools, and waterbeds. If the water supply to your home is disrupted, you can retain and use the water in your hot water heater. Hot water heaters usually contain 15 to 40 gallons of water. Simply open the drain faucet at the bottom of the heater. The water may need to be filtered before using it. Hot water heaters are the best source of potable (drinkable) water. You can also obtain drinking water by melting any ice in your freezer.

Toilet tanks contain 5 to 7 gallons of water. This water should be boiled for at least 10 minutes before using it. If you clean your toilet by putting a liquid dispenser or chemical tablet in the tank, then this water cannot be used. Water in toilet bowls should not be used by people, but can be used to provide water for pets.

Waterbed water is normally treated with a chemical solution to prevent algae growth. This water should not be used for drinking, but can be used for washing if it is boiled first. Swimming pool water can also be used if boiled.

Water Purification

Another item you need to include in your emergency preparedness storeroom is a water purification system. Water obtained from springs, ponds, lakes, and rivers contains contaminants in the form of microorganisms (bacteria, viruses, parasites), toxic minerals and metals, and chemicals. Drinking contaminated water can cause physical disruption as minor as a stomach ache, and as major as death. If you are not positive about the purity of the water you are drinking or cooking with, you must purify it before use. On the next page is a chart describing various methods for purifying water, along with their advantages and disadvantages.

Chapter 4 — Water Basics

Water Purification Alternatives

Method	Benefits	Result	Drawbacks
Boiling	• Inexpensive • Simple • Quick	• Kills bacteria and microorganisms • Does not filter sediment	• Uses cooking fuel • Experts disagree on length of time water must be boiled. Most say at least 10 minutes at rolling boil. • Water may taste flat after boiling.
Disinfecting with Commercial Household Bleach (add 2 drops per quart for clear water and double the amount for cloudy water, stir thoroughly, let stand for 30 minutes.)	• Simple • Inexpensive • No special equipment is required.	• Kills viruses, organisms, and bacteria. • If done correctly, this method will leave a chlorine bleach odor in the treated water. • Does not remove sediment.	• Some experts believe bleach is toxic to humans when ingested in large quantities. • This method does not eliminate potentially harmful chemicals in water.
Disinfecting with 2% Tincture of Iodine (3 drops per quart for clear water, double the amount for cloudy water.)	• Simple • Inexpensive	• Same results as purification with bleach.	• Water will have peculiar odor and taste. • Can be harmful to people who consume too much or who have thyroid problems.
Aerobic oxygen (10 drops per quart for purifying, 5 drops per quart for keeping stored water healthy)	• Simple • No special equipment is required.	• Removes chlorine from water. • Kills microorganisms.	• Expensive ($20 for a 2 oz. bottle that will purify 60 gallons of water) • Does not remove sediment.
Water filters and purifiers	• Removes sediment • Trap organisms and bacteria of various sizes (depending on filter) • Can remove chemicals if carbon filter is used.	• Removes everything but the smallest viruses unless iodine additive (purifier) is used.	• Expensive ($70-$300, extra parts $19-$75) • Prone to clogging • Requires replacement filters and parts. • Filter a limited amount of water.

Chapter 4   *Water Basics*

Making water safe for drinking can be a complicated process. Be sure you have a large teakettle that can be used over an open flame for heating and purifying water. Also, add chlorine bleach to your household storage list. Our family was fortunate to be able to afford to purchase a water filtration system and a replacement filter. We purchased the best one we could afford. If you decide to obtain one yourself, you can talk to people at a preparedness supply or mountaineering store. Many different sizes, options, and prices are available. One thing we discovered is that many of the water filters and purifiers on the market are able to filter thousands of gallons of water. If your financial resources are limited, you may want to talk to your neighbors and procure one purification system for several households. If you have unlimited financial resources, you will want to buy a few of these in case one of them breaks, clogs, or fails.

Sources for Water Storage and/or Purification Supplies

Company	Telephone	Web Site	Address
The Country Store Preparedness Center	(888) 311-8940	www.healthyharvest.com	11013 A NE 39th St. Vancouver, WA 98662
Christian Family Resources	(719) 962-3228 Monday-Friday 1-5 p.m. MST	N/A Send $2 for catalog to PO Box	PO Box 405 Kit Carson, CO 80825
Emergency Essentials	(800) 999-1863	www.beprepared.com	165 S. Mountain Way Drive Orem, UT 84058
Happy Hovel Storable Foods	(800) 637-7772	www.wwmagic.com	PO Box 781 Yelm, WA 98597
H&W Distributors	(888) 301-8307	www.zianet.com/hwd	316 E. Hall St., Box 859 Hatch, NM 87937
Jade Mountain	(800) 442-1972	www.jademountain.com	PO Box 4616 Boulder, CO 80306-4616
Mountain Magic	(800) 979-2665	www.mtn-magic.com	12371 W. 64th Ave. Arvada, CO 80004
Ready Made Resources	(800) 627-3809	www.cococo.net/rmr	239 Cagle Road Tellico Plains, TN 37385
River Valley Outfitters	(501) 474-6313	N/A	PO Box 1248 724 Main Street Van Buren, AR 72957
Survival Products	(215) 722-7797	N/A	7975 Oxford Avenue Philadelphia, PA 19111

Disclaimer: *This list was compiled for your convenience. It does not guarantee the availability or quality of products or suppliers, nor is it a complete list of potential suppliers. As information changes over time, this list may not be accurate. Conduct your own research before purchasing products.*

Water Action Plan

Level 1	Person Responsible	Due Date	✓
Water Storage			
Identify Storage Space(s) for Water			
Determine Minimum # of Gallons			
Buy Water Storage Containers			
Buy Bung Wrench to Open Barrels			
Buy Siphon Pump (1)			
Set Aside Reusable Containers			
Clean Storage Containers			
Obtain Shelves or Pallets			
Fill Containers with Clean Water			
Water Retention and Transportation			
Clean Roof and Rain Gutters			
Buy Gutter Siphons			
Buy Downspout Hose			
Buy or Make Retention Tank			
Look for Water Sources Near Home			
Buy 5 gallon Portable Jug(s)			
Obtain Hand Truck or Wheelbarrow			
Water Purification			
Buy and Store Chlorine Bleach			
Buy Water Filter or Purifier			
Buy Replacement Parts			
Test Operation of Filter/Purifier			
Level 2 (Level 1 Plus)			
Purchase Both Filter and Purifier			
Store 60 Gallons Per Person			
Level 3 (Level 1 and 2 Plus)			
Live on Property with Own Well			
Purchase Diesel Generator for Pump			
Have Backup Manual Pump System			

I signify that the Water Preparedness Activities are complete.
Our Household Has Successfully Taken Action to Prepare for a Grid Failure or Natural Disaster

_____
Signed

_____
Date

Food Preparation

"Moooommmmyyyy!!!!!"

I hear Katie shrieking on the front porch, drop the laundry I'm folding, and race outside.

"What's wrong?"

"Jenny won't play with me anymore," Katie sobs, tears gushing down her cheeks.

Jenny Wilson lives two doors down from us, and is Katie's best friend.

"Why won't Jenny play with you?" I asked, assuming it involves some normal, five-year-old type dispute over Beanie Babies or Barbie clothes.

"Because our family has pock lips," cries Katie.

"What are pock lips?"

"Jenny's mommy says our family has pock lips, and she's not supposed to play with me anymore."

Pock lips, pock lips, apocalypse. The Wilsons must think we have lost our minds over Y2K, and are predicting an apocalypse. Oh boy. The joys of parenting.

Chapter 5   Food Preparation

"I tell you what, honey. I will talk to Jenny's mom. Don't worry about it. I have a feeling Jenny's parents will change their minds. You have so many other friends you can play with today. Let's wash your hands for lunch, and I'll work this out with the Wilsons."

One of the challenges Anne, Al, and I have encountered as we've begun to do research on the millennium bug, and to talk to our friends and neighbors about it, is that people react in many different ways. They also change their feelings from one day to the next. Sometimes they want to talk with us about all we've learned and what they can do to prepare. An hour later, they want to think we've lost our minds, and avoid every news clip they see on Y2K. And, when they're in that mode of not wanting to think about it, they certainly don't feel like spending time with us.

What most people don't realize is that we have experienced all of the same doubts, fears, hopes, and fluctuations in belief that they have. I've often asked myself why I'm taking so much time to write this book, and why I'm putting every spare dollar we have into our preparedness effort. This summer, we could be buying new tires and skis, shopping for a bigger TV, or going on vacation like many of our friends and neighbors. Instead, we're budgeting, saving, cutting, and planning - our new recreational activity is Y2K and emergency preparedness. We've also warned Ben that he won't be skiing at all this winter. I still don't think he believes us, but it's true. Our priorities have changed.

When I start to feel like this isn't real, like it isn't going to be a big deal, like I can't imagine living without television, indoor plumbing, and a fully stocked grocery store - the temptation is to live in denial and just procrastinate or not think about it. "Let's just enjoy every minute until the infrastructure caves. Live for the moment, party on...." And then, the responsible side of me takes over, the part that faces challenges head on. Our family is fortunate. We understand what might happen. New articles are appearing every day talking about the potential severity of Y2K. Even though it is tempting to not think about it and not talk about it, deep down, I know that we all need to prepare as well as we can.

So, I'll speak with Janet Wilson and try to explain that we aren't insane, negative, gloom and doom people. Maybe I can persuade her to store a little food and water. I wish she would have called me before telling Jenny to stop playing with Katie. But, she's probably heard rumors about how we've converted our basement into a warehouse, and how we are having drills with our kids on how to live without electricity. Actually, if I was in her shoes, and hadn't spent the last four months doing research, I'd probably think people who are doing what we're doing are a little crazy, too. She probably thinks she's protecting her children by sheltering them from what might happen. Interesting...

Cooking without Electricity

I'll never forget the first time I saw a microwave oven. We were visiting the Home Economics laboratory at Colorado State University. It was in the early 1970's. They had this huge, industrial looking, heavy metal machine that was imbedded in a concrete wall. It had lots of weird looking gauges and knobs, and looked like it would be used for a medical experiment. The people in the lab were trying to figure out how to bake a cake in thirty seconds. I wondered why anyone would want to bake a cake that fast. Now, it is difficult to imagine living without my little microwave.

When we were kids, my grandmother used to cook everything from scratch - bread, noodles, cookies, and spaghetti sauce. I remember she'd fix breakfast, then wash and dry the dishes. Then, we'd have an hour or so to play hide and seek with her, or dress up in satin nightgowns and lipstick and jewelry. Then, she'd cook lunch and do the dishes. By the time we took a nap and played a quick game of cards or checkers, she'd be starting dinner. My mother, on the other

Chapter 5 — Food Preparation

hand, bought things like pasta, bread, and desserts already made. But, she would still devote at least an hour of her time each night preparing dinner. And, if we ate pizza every few weeks, or went out for a hamburger, she felt guilty. Times have really changed. Today, unless it is a special occasion, I rarely spend more than thirty minutes fixing a meal.

The reality of preparing food without running water or electricity is that it will be time consuming and labor intensive compared to what we are used to. Cooking without electricity will require us to relearn ways of cooking that even grandma may have forgotten. The process we use in the 90's to get a meal on the table is much different than it was twenty years ago. Using microwave ovens and easy-to-prepare food products have made our kitchens efficient in the same way that upgrading from typewriters to word processors streamlined document production.

Because most of us aren't accustomed to cooking from scratch, conserving heat, and using only two burners, our family decided to practice using our storage food and stove. In the beginning, every Friday night, we'd make dinner using our alternative stove and basic foods. The rules were that we couldn't use indoor plumbing such as running water, the garbage disposal, indoor drains, or electricity to make or clean up after the meal. Now, we have worked up to staging back-to-basics weekends and living without modern conveniences one weekend a month.

We've learned that preparing meals the old-fashioned way becomes easier with the proper tools, planning, and reasonable expectations. Since we had already replaced all of our electrical kitchen appliances with their manual equivalents (when a manual alternative was available), we had most of the tools we needed. If you haven't cooked with basic ingredients like powdered milk, powdered cheese, rice, beans, etc., you will probably need a few cookbooks. A series of cookbooks we like that provide simple recipes have been written by nutritionist Peggy Layton. They are available at preparedness stores, by calling (435) 835-0311, or by writing to: PO Box 44 Manti, Utah 84642. Another great basic cookbook, that covers just about everything, is *Joy of Cooking* (Irma Rombauer and Marion Rombauer Becker). It is sold at most retail bookstores.

One thing we hadn't really anticipated is how complicated it would be to haul water. We used water from our drinking supply in the basement, or our rainwater supply on the back porch. Water is heavy and sloshes when you carry it. After our first experimental dinner, we bought a large enamelware soup pot with a lid, and used it to transport drinking water. We also got several galvanized steel buckets for transporting clean washing water. Managing water usage is more efficient when we use dish pans in both sinks for washing and rinsing dishes. We also discovered it is easier to pour in hot water first, then add cold until it is the correct temperature. This helps conserve the hot water. After we wash and rinse the dishes, the old wash water is discarded, and the rinsing water saved to be used for wash water next time.

Lighting our stove requires matches. We have thoroughly stocked up on wooden kitchen matches, and found an old-fashioned, wall mounted matchbox holder at a flea market to hang by the stove. This keeps matches safe, dry, and handy. A glass jar would work just as well. When you buy kitchen matches in the big boxes, buy more than you think you will ever need. They are also required to light lanterns and candles, and we have been amazed at how many matches we use during our back-to-basics weekends without electricity.

Cooking on two burners and trying to save fuel poses a few challenges. First of all, you need to have everything chopped, mixed, and ready to go into the pan before you ever heat up the stove. That way, you don't cook your ingredients any longer than you absolutely need to. We received a set of various sized heavy glass mixing bowls from a friend who found them in the *Lillian Vernon* catalog. Anne said she's seen some like them at department stores and cookware shops. The bowls range in size from very large to very small, so you can use the size you need and save counter space.

Chapter 5 *Food Preparation*

Another interesting phenomenon about cooking on a two burner stove is that the way you serve food may change. Normally, at the extremely informal Olsen residence, everyone grabs a dinner plate and serves themselves from pans on the stove. And, if people want seconds and the food has cooled down, they simply put it in the microwave. When we prepare meals on the propane stove, we only want to heat the food once so we can conserve cooking fuel. So, we transfer the food to casserole dishes with lids to help it stay warm.

Al discovered another great way to keep food warm longer. He found some insulated containers that look like big cloth lunch boxes, and can keep food hot or cold for hours. They are available at sporting goods stores, or by mail order from *High Street Emporium*, and sell for about $30-$40 each, depending on the size. We also found some less expensive models ($12-$18) at our membership warehouse, next to the plastic camping coolers.

We can use these high-tech insulators to keep hot food warmer, and we can put snow in them (when available) and use them to keep our milk cold. We purchased an inexpensive powdered milk mixing pitcher from our preparedness food company. It mixes the milk using a special plunger in the lid, so the milk is smoother and better tasting. We mix enough milk for one meal with our warm storage water, and then put it in the cooler an hour or so before we plan to eat. Sometimes we add some vanilla extract or chocolate syrup to sweeten the taste.

On our first experimental cooking night, we faced another sobering reality. Without the use of a refrigerator or a garbage disposal, leftovers were a problem. We could either feed them to Cisco or compost them. It is best to use the compost bin for things like vegetable peels. And, we prefer that Cisco eat only dog food. With practice, we are learning to estimate accurately, and to only fix what we'll eat. This is especially challenging with children. Our kids have never lived with the "clean your plate" rule we grew up with. For years, I've been guilty of throwing away that extra serving of green beans, macaroni and cheese, or canned soup that the kids didn't feel like eating. Those foods were inexpensive, so we could just buy more. After facing the prospect of throwing away precious food from our emergency storage, we have come up with a new philosophy about how much food to cook. If we aren't sure, we prepare **less** than we think we will eat, and then make popcorn later if everyone is still hungry. I can honestly say, we have a new appreciation for every meal we eat. We hope we never take food for granted again.

Stoves

If you are a person who likes to cook, you probably have a special relationship with your stove. The type of stove you have now, and the types of fuel you are legally permitted to burn in your home, will probably influence the type of alternative stove you use. We have a gas stove in our kitchen. It operates on natural gas from our public utility company, and it will operate on propane with an adapter. Although it has an electric ignition device that lights the burners, it does not require electricity to operate. I can simply turn on a burner and light it with a match, and it will work. If you have a gas stove that uses electricity for things like a clock or igniters, unplug it, and then see whether your oven will heat, and if gas flows to your burners. Some gas stoves will not operate at all without electricity because they use electricity to regulate the gas flow. If your stove will operate without electricity, the question is - if the electrical grid goes down, will we still have natural gas? The answer is, it depends.

Last winter, the power went off in our subdivision because of a severe snow storm. We still had natural gas, and could use our stove. Even though our neighborhood was without power, other people in the Denver metro area had electricity, the emergency 911 system worked, and so did most telephones. In the Year 2000 scenario, conceivably, a community's entire electrical system could be inoperative, impacting telephones, emergency services, etc. In that case, the public

Chapter 5 *Food Preparation*

utility would probably turn off the natural gas system for safety reasons. No one really knows what will happen, so we decided to be prepared to cook with fuel other than natural gas.

When considering which type of stove to buy, you will want to consider your budget, available storage space, and the number of people you will be cooking for. You will also need to consider the safety of using particular types of stoves indoors. Carbon monoxide can be generated by any gas or fuel powered appliance including wood and gas stoves, fireplaces, and heaters. Charcoal barbecue grills produce especially high amounts of carbon monoxide, and should never be used indoors. Purchasing a battery-powered carbon monoxide detector is a good idea. You should also own a fire extinguisher, and have baking soda or a bucket of sand near your stove.

Unless you live in an area which permits wood burning, and have lots of storage space and money, you will probably not be using a wood cook stove. Cooking with wood will be discussed later. For an emergency stove, the non-electric stoves designed for camping will probably meet the needs of most families. They are available in different sizes, weights, and price ranges. They differ in quality, durability, and ease of use. The best way to buy a stove is to visit a camping, mountaineering, or preparedness supply store. Then you can see the stove; learn how to refuel and light it; understand the fuel requirements; and compare various models and brands.

Here are some considerations when buying a stove for emergency use:

1. How much heat does the stove produce?
   Heat output is measured in btus (British thermal units). The higher the number, the more heat. If you want to use your stove as a heat source, this is important.

2. How many burners does the stove have?
   If you plan to use the stove to prepare meals every day, consider a stove with two burners. Dual burner stoves are also able to accommodate griddles and stove-top ovens.

3. How stable and durable is the stove?
   For household use, it will be important to have a stove which doesn't tip over easily, and which is sturdy enough to tolerate daily usage for a month or more.

4. What type of fuel does the stove use?
   Considerations for fuel are: availability, shelf life, storage requirements, and type of receptacle used. Some stoves are capable of burning more than one type of fuel. Stoves which use disposable canisters will require you to figure out how to get rid of empty canisters. Fuel which can be safely stored in your house is preferable, especially if you do not have a garage.

5. How fuel efficient is the stove?
   Remember, your stove will be used for cooking as well as heating water for washing and drinking. To be safe, you should plan on burning your stove using medium heat for at least 3 to 5 hours per day. The amount of fuel required to burn for 100 to 150 hours, and the cost of replacement fuel are important considerations.

6. What is required to light, refuel, and repair the stove?
   Ease of operation is an often overlooked factor when purchasing this type of stove. Try to purchase a stove which doesn't require open flame priming. Also, look at the replacement parts and tool kits available for maintaining the stove.

Chapter 5 Food Preparation

7. What type of environments and locations can the stove be safely used in?
   Can the stove be operated in a house, a tent, or outdoors only? Does the stove require special ventilation or piping?

We decided to buy a propane adapter for our big gas stove. We then went to our membership warehouse and purchased some small propane tanks like the ones we use on our barbecue grill. They cost about $25 a piece. Al had them filled with propane, and they will be used to run our big stove if we lose our inflow of natural gas. We also have a small, portable camp stove that will burn gas in small canisters or unleaded gasoline. We'll have some fuel for it, just in case. Camp stoves cost less - about $40 and up, and burn fuel from bottles, or from propane tanks, with an adapter. The stoves and fuel are usually available at camping and mountaineering stores, or from any store that sells camping supplies, like Target, Wal-Mart, or Kmart. Anne has an electric stove in her house, and doesn't own a camping stove, so she decided to splurge. Her two burner stove will run off of propane or natural gas, with the appropriate adapters. It is well made and sturdy. She paid $180 dollars for the stove, and about $35 for the propane adapter. She is also storing several propane tanks.

If you live in a wooded area, or in a place where you are permitted to burn wood, you can heat your house and boil water on a wood stove designed for heating. Prices range from approximately $500 to $2000. Or, you can purchase a new wood cook stove for between $700 and $3000. Used wood stoves can be bought for much less. Wood cook stoves enable you to regulate the cooking temperature and to vary the temperature for each burner. Most have ovens, and some have receptacles for heating hot water. All wood stoves require chimneys and special maintenance. They also require you to take precautions so you will not burn your house down. If you intend to cook with a wood stove, two good books on the subject are Anita Evangelista's - *How to Live without Electricity and Like It* (1997, Loompanics Unlimited, Port Townsend, WA) and Carla Emery's - *Encyclopedia of Country Living* (1994, Sasquatch Books, Seattle, WA). These books are easy to read and contain phenomenal amounts of information about living without electricity and running water. They are available at book stores, preparedness stores, and from *amazon.com* on the Worldwide Web.

How much wood you will need will depend on how much cooking you do, how well insulated your house is, how cold it is outside, and how warm you need to be. For cooking only, you will need to plan on using two armloads of wood per day. We will discuss heating with wood in more detail in Chapter 6.

Ovens

If you plan to cook on a two burner stove designed for camping, and would like the ability to roast and bake, you may want to consider buying a camping or solar oven. Camping ovens are metal boxes with handles that sit on top of a wood stove or camp stove. Depending on the size (one or two burners wide), they range in price from approximately $70 to $150. On a sunny day, solar ovens are a non-polluting alternative to stove-top ovens. The best ones sell for approximately $200. You can build your own solar oven, if you are so inclined. The resource table at the end of the chapter will tell you where to obtain instructions.

Cookware

When selecting cookware, conserving fuel is a key consideration. Two types of pans that are especially efficient are those made from cast iron, and woks; both retain and distribute heat efficiently. The best pots and pans to use will have metal handles, instead of plastic or wood,

Chapter 5 — Food Preparation

which can melt or burn when exposed to an open flame. Non-flammable rubber or leather covers can be purchased for metal handles.

Cast iron pans are excellent for boiling, frying, heating, and even baking, and are extremely durable. When you first use a new cast iron pan, you will need to "cure" it with oil. They also must be hand dried after washing to prevent rusting. Cast iron is extremely durable. Used pans are better than new ones. You may be able to buy cast iron cookware at garage sales, estate auctions, or used dry good stores run by *Good Will* or the *Salvation Army*. We've also found it at grocery stores, discount stores, and camping stores. Cast iron is available by mail order, however, it is very heavy and shipping charges can add up.

Many preparedness experts agree that if you are only going to have one pan for cooking in an emergency, it should be a cast iron Dutch oven. Dutch ovens are round, deep pots with metal handles over the top, and strong lids. Some have small legs for standing in a campfire. If you've ever watched a western movie with a covered wagon cook scene, the pan they ladle the beans out of is a Dutch oven. Dutch ovens are durable and versatile. A metal handle enables the pot to be hung over a fire on special camp irons, or in a fireplace. These pots can be used on top of the stove for soups and stews, or can be buried in coals and used to bake bread.

In addition to basics such as small and large frying pans, small and large sauce pans, and a large soup kettle, you may consider purchasing a cast iron griddle. It can be used for making pancakes and tortillas. You will also need a kettle for heating water. Using cast iron or aluminum kettles for drinking water is not recommended because the water takes on a metallic taste. When buying kettles, keep in mind you can use them for boiling water for washing, bathing, etc., as well as for purifying drinking water and making coffee and tea. Buy the biggest, most durable kettle you can find. You can also use an enamel coffee pot to heat water. These are inexpensive and available where camping supplies are sold.

If you already own gourmet cookware - such as Calphalon™ or Magnalite Professional™, these pans will work fine. They have metal handles and retain heat well. Just make sure you have lots of heavy duty pot holders handy.

Woks are efficient because they provide more surface area on which to cook food than traditional frying pans do. They are especially designed for stir frying meat and vegetables, and can also be used to steam foods. The best selection of reasonably priced woks are found in Chinatown in San Francisco or New York, but they are also readily available at specialty cookware stores, and at import stores such as *Cost Plus Imports* or *Pier One*. They can also be found at Asian grocery stores. Cast iron woks are available, but are heavy to maneuver. We recommend a basic steel wok. Most woks have wooden handles, so you'll need to be careful when using them over open flame. Metal frying utensils are a good idea to have, and can be purchased inexpensively where woks are sold. We will note here that our menus for Level 1 do not require a wok. However, we recommend this type of cooking for those pursuing a healthy and self-sufficient lifestyle. If you decide to grow a vegetable garden, you'll find that nothing beats stir-fried, home grown vegetables over rice, so get a wok - and stock up on rice, soy sauce, and sesame oil.

Another way to conserve fuel is to prepare foods such as beans and rice, which take a while to cook, in a pressure cooker. My grandmother used a pressure cooker regularly. The pressure cookers available today are safer than those grandma used. Many people prefer using pressure cookers because they reduce cooking time by as much as 30%, and help retain nutrients in food. If you decide to buy a pressure cooker, make sure you obtain replacement parts such as rubber gaskets and gauges. Also, read the directions carefully. For more information on pressure cookers, visit a retail store near you that specializes in cooking supplies.

Chapter 5　　　　　　　　　　　　　　　　　　　Food Preparation

One additional thought about cookware and cooking utensils: for those of you who don't cook regularly, or who don't use many fresh fruits and vegetables, be sure to take an inventory of your knife collection. Having a complete set of high quality, sharp knives makes all the difference in the world when cooking from scratch. Cutting food with sharp knives is much safer than using a dull knife. Be sure you have a sturdy, non-electric knife sharpener in your kitchen, as well.

Living without a Refrigerator

The easiest way to prepare for living without your refrigerator is to simply eliminate the need for refrigeration. If you live in a place where it snows, or if you have a creek on your property, you will be able to keep food cool easier. A little known fact to people who haven't ever lived in Colorado, is that many times during the winter, we will have sunny days with temperatures over 60 degrees. So, our family knows we can't plan to have snow and ice available for keeping food cold, even in January.

Today, we use our refrigerator to preserve fresh foods such as vegetables and milk, and to keep leftovers cold for reuse. If the grid goes down, we won't have fresh food unless it comes from a garden. We discussed earlier how we can cook to reduce the amount of leftovers. Some leftovers can actually be stored without refrigeration, although most Americans aren't aware of this. Anne lived with a Chinese family one summer, and was appalled to discover that they put leftover cooked rice in a covered bowl, and left it out on the counter top until they used it the next day. Cooked rice is one food that can safely be stored for several days without refrigeration.

Fortunately, no one in our family requires prescription medicines to survive. Some medical conditions require daily access to refrigerated medication. If someone in your family needs medication that must be refrigerated, you should buy a refrigerator that runs on alternative fuel such as propane or kerosene. They are expensive, ranging in price from $500 to $1500, and can be purchased from companies like *Lehman's* in Kidron, Ohio (a supplier of many products used by Amish families). They are also available from *Kansas Wind Power*. See the source table on page 111 for contact information.

We plan to be able to live without refrigeration, and then if it snows, and we want to put leftovers in a cooler with some snow, we can. On snowy days, we'll also be able to cook things like beans, soups, and stews in larger quantities and save cooking fuel. One of the toughest things to adjust to will be drinking warm milk. We decided to buy an old-fashioned ceramic water crock that keeps water cooler than room temperature and doesn't require electricity. It isn't as cold as refrigerated water, but it isn't warm, either. Anyone who has traveled overseas knows that most Americans are obsessed with having ice in their beverages. We have German friends who refuse to let us consume iced drinks in front of them when they visit us. They believe strongly that drinking cold liquids is not healthy, and they regularly consume lukewarm water, beer, and tea. So, whenever we are faced with drinking warm milk, we'll just think of our European friends, and remind ourselves how beneficial the practice is.

Root Cellaring, Drying, and Canning

If you are using this book to prepare for a one month utility grid failure, then you probably just need to get a camp stove, some fuel, and a few extra pots and pans, and you'll be all set. If, however, you are planning to grow a garden or buy fruits and vegetables from the farmer's market to supplement your food supply, you will want to consider other methods of preserving food.

Chapter 5   Food Preparation

Root cellaring can be done in an underground cellar or a basement. Root crops such as carrots, onions, garlic, potatoes, and turnips are ideal for this type of storage. Winter squash, pumpkins, cabbage, and green tomatoes also store well.

Dehydration is a method that has been used for centuries to preserve fruits, vegetables, and herbs. For approximately $40, you can purchase a solar dehydrator that will dry food using the energy of the sun, without electricity. The drying pantry protects food from dust, and can also be used to grow sprouts.

Canning is an art as well as a science. It is time consuming, and requires special equipment and knowledge. Only fruits and tomatoes can be water bath canned. Low-acidity vegetables and meats require the higher temperatures achieved through pressure canning. If you want to start canning, and have never done it before, do some research. Read books and look over some brochures from canning supply companies. If you can, go through the canning process the first few times with someone who is experienced. Think of a friend or relative of yours with the biggest vegetable garden, and ask if they need any help canning.

To Grind or Not to Grind

Feeding a family without electricity seems a little overwhelming. Since we began conducting our weekend without electricity drills, we've found that the process is actually kind of fun, and that food made from scratch tastes better. Speaking of food made from scratch, we want to take this opportunity to talk a little bit about storing grains like wheat and corn and grinding your own flour.

When we talked to people who are committed to storing food and preparing for emergencies, we discovered that most of them store whole grains, and grind their own flour. There are two basic reasons for this - grains can be stored much longer than other foods, and freshly ground grains have lots more nutritional value than commercially processed flours and cereals. If you decide you want to grind your own flour, buy some bulk wheat flour at a health food store, and bake fresh bread for your family for a while to test everyone's tolerance to wheat . Some people are allergic to wheat, and don't realize it until they regularly begin eating freshly ground grains.

Grinding your own flour requires that you purchase wheat and a grain mill. We recommend a mill that doesn't require electricity. Grain mills can be purchased from stores that specialize in bread making, or from preparedness food suppliers.

We use our mill to make wheat flour, corn meal, and cereal. We also learned to bake bread. Ben and Katie used to whine if we asked them to eat wheat bread. Now, they actually prefer the flavor and richness of homemade wheat bread, and complain if we try to give them white bread from the grocery store.

Food Preparation Supplies - Mail Order Sources

Item	Source	Contact Information	✓
Non-Electric Stoves	*Cabela's*	Call (800) 237-4444 for catalog or visit www.cabelas.com	
	Lehman's Non-Electric Catalog	Send $3 for catalog to: PO Box 41 Kidron, Ohio 44636 (330) 857-5757 or visit www.Lehmans.com	
	REI	Visit www.rei.com or look for a retail store near you	
Solar Ovens Instructions to Build	*James Dulley*	www.dulley.com or write to: PO Box 54987 Cincinnati, OH 45254	
Sources to Purchase	*Jade Mountain*	www.jademountain.com (800) 442-1972 PO Box 4616 Boulder, CO 80306-4616	
	Kansas Wind Power	Send $4 for Catalog to: 13569 214th Road Holton, KS 66436-8138	
	Real Goods	www.realgoods.com (800) 762-7325 555 Leslie Street Ukiah, CA 95482-5576	
Cast Iron Cookware	*Cumberland General Store*	www.cumberlandgeneral.com or Send $4 for Catalog to: #1 Highway 68 Crossville, TN 38555 (800) 334-4640	
	Lehman's	www.Lehmans.com or Send $3 for catalog to: PO Box 41 Kidron, Ohio 44636 (330) 857-5757	
	Modern Farm	www.modfarm.com (800) 443-4934 1825 Big Horn Avenue Cody, WY 82414	
Solar Food Dryer Instructions to Build	*James Dulley* Sun-Wood-Wind Handbook 1997 by James. T. Dulley	www.dulley.com or write to: PO Box 54987 Cincinnati, OH 45254	
	Real Goods	See Listing Above	
Sources to Purchase	*Jade Mountain*	See Listing Above	

Disclaimer: This list was compiled for your convenience. It does not guarantee the availability or quality of products or suppliers, nor is it a complete list of potential suppliers. As information changes over time, this list may not be accurate. Conduct your own research before purchasing products.

Food Preparation Action Plan

Level 1	Person Responsible	Due Date	✓
Kitchen Supplies			
Containers for Hauling Water			
Complete Knife Set			
Manual Knife Sharpener			
Fireproof Oven Mitts			
Stove			
Portable Stove			
Fuel Containers and Fuel			
Kitchen Matches			
Fire Extinguisher			
Stove Repair Tools/Parts			
Cookware			
Dutch Oven(s)			
Frying Pan			
Water Heating Kettle and/or Pot			
Bread and Muffin Pans			
Food Preservation			
Ice Chest or Cooler			
Level 2 (Level 1 Plus)			
Wok			
Griddle			
Extra Fuel			
Extra Mixing Bowls			
Extra Storage Containers			
Camp Oven			
Level 3 (Level 1 Plus)			
Grain Mill			
Canning Supplies			
Solar Dehydrator			
Solar Oven			
Camp Irons for Over Fire Cooking			
Pressure Cooker			
Build a Root Cellar			

I signify that the Food Preparation Preparedness Activities are complete. Our Household Has Successfully Taken Action to Prepare for a Grid Failure or Natural Disaster

_____
Signed

_____
Date

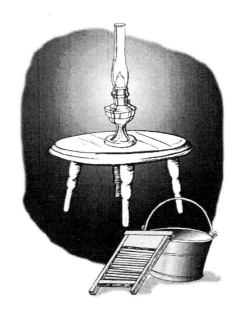

Light, Heat, Washing, and Waste

What could be a better test of living with a grid failure than to just try to function without electricity? It was a Friday night, and after dinner, Al shut off the fuse box switches for everything except the refrigerator, the chest freezer, and the hot water heater. We made a family pact that the electricity would stay off until Sunday night at 8:00. That would give us time to reset clocks and get ready for school on Monday.

At the time, it seemed like a great idea. Looking back, our test could have used a bit more planning. But, as you know, hindsight is 20/20.

Actually, it wasn't too bad at first. We were sitting in the living room in complete darkness in front of our newly purchased Aladdin lamp. An Aladdin lamp is a wonderful invention. It looks like the old-fashioned oil lamps grandma used to have, except that it has a mantle like a camping lantern, that puts out up to 60 watts of light. We had purchased an aluminum model with a fuel filler plug on the base, so we wouldn't need to disassemble the lamp to add kerosene. I was elected to light the lamp. In our commitment to authenticity, we had closed our curtains so outside light wouldn't come into the house.

Sitting in pitch black darkness, it occurred to me that I would probably burn the house down if I tried to light this thing in the dark. Lesson one, we need to have flashlights handy in every room that requires a lamp to be lit. Next, we realized that the matches were in the kitchen, buried in a drawer. I asked Ben to run out into the garage and get the camping flashlight.

"Make Dad do it," he moaned.

Chapter 6   Light, Heat, Washing, and Waste

Much to my surprise, my macho ten year old son is afraid of the dark. After a short debate, I groped my way into the kitchen, scrounged for matches, lit a taper candle in a tall candleholder from the dining room table, and used it to light the Aladdin. Replacing the chimney was tricky, because it got hot so quickly. The lamp, we discovered, generates a tremendous amount of heat. Flammable materials such as magazines, books, and cloth table coverings had to be moved away from the lamp after lighting it.

We realized that, in the future, it would be a good idea to have a flashlight in the room when we lit the lamp. So, we'd be prepared for the next time, I decided to go and find a flashlight. Carrying the candle, I went upstairs. During the entire episode, I was terrified the candle would fall out of the holder and set my carpet on fire. I finally located a flashlight buried in the bottom of the junk drawer in the den. Lesson two - when buying candles, buy short squatty ones that fit in portable candle holders. Better yet, hang a small flashlight around everyone's neck, and make sure you have rechargeable batteries for them.

We decided to institute a policy that flames would only be transported by adults. Although we want our kids to be self sufficient, they simply haven't had enough experience to respect and baby-sit a lit flame. Also, we realized that dogs and small kids bump into tables. Lit lamps and candles must be placed on sturdy, stable surfaces, away from draperies, paper, and anything else likely to burst into flames.

At this point, Katie decided she needed to go to the bathroom. I was not too surprised that my five year old saw boogie men in every shadow, and had considered wetting her pants instead of facing them. I could see the potential for a month of holding my child by the hand after dark unless I instituted a compromise. Al ran out to the garage for the big flashlight, and I gave Katie the small one. I told her I'd take her this time, but next time, her ferocious guard dog, Cisco, would have to go with her. We already had placed candles in our bathroom, so I went in, lit one in the corner, and sent Katie in alone with her flashlight. She cried a little at first, but we managed to get through the first bathroom visit alive.

Since our favorite family game is Jenga, Al had set it up in the middle of the coffee table. Jenga is a game with small stacking wood pieces. Each person takes a turn and tries to pull an individual piece out of the pile and place it on the top without bringing down the tower. Lesson three - smart survivalists don't put lit flames near toppling towers. Play cards or board games at night. Save the construction games for daylight.

Fortunately, we had Anne duplicate our test in her apartment. She faired much better. She had practiced lighting her lamp several times in broad daylight before she tried it with limited light. She also had purchased some receptacles to hold large and small kitchen matches, and had strategically placed them in each room. In her living room, she lit a candle mounted in a wall sconce with a chimney, so that she could have a centrally located light. She is just so darned capable... But, more about our weekend preparedness drills in the next chapter.

Let There Be Light

In the event that you lose your electricity, there are numerous options for lighting inside your home. These include - flashlights, candles, oil lamps, kerosene, and battery powered lamps. If you choose any option that requires fire - candles, kerosene, or oil lamps, keep two things in mind. First, for safety reasons, be sure you have a fire extinguisher and operational smoke detector. Second, stock up on lots of matches. You will be amazed at how much you use them.

Chapter 6 — Light, Heat, Washing, and Waste

Moving burning candles from room to room is just not practical. We outfitted everyone in our family with a flashlight to hang around their neck. During our preparedness weekend drills, we all pop them on at dusk. They are kind of fun for the kids because they look cool, and hanging them around your neck prevents them from being misplaced or lost. Most of the smaller flashlights on the market have rings for hanging. We chose the size that uses AA batteries (we use rechargeables and a solar charger). A flashlight will run for approximately 8 hours on a set of batteries. We also got a few replacement bulbs.

One thing to consider if you live in a multi-level dwelling such as an apartment building is that you will probably be carrying things up and down dark stairwells. You will definitely want to purchase a head lamp flashlight so you can keep you hands free if you need to haul water, garbage, etc. Even during the day, stairwells in buildings are usually dark. You should buy the most durable model you can find. Head lamp flashlights can be purchased for about $15 wherever flashlights are sold. Be sure you include batteries for all of your flashlights in your battery inventory (*Chapter 2*).

For ambient lighting when you don't need to read or see in fine detail, candles work well. The bigger around the candle is, and the higher quality the wax, the longer it will burn. Standard taper candles like most of us use on our dining room tables should burn about thirty minutes per inch. Candles an inch in diameter should burn about an hour per inch. Most large candles used for decoration list a maximum burn time on the package. The larger the candle is in diameter, the greater the burn time per inch. Candles will burn more slowly if they are inside a glass chimney, protected from draughts. Burning candles for a maximum of two hours, then letting them cool before lighting again, will actually help them last longer. If you have limited storage space, you can purchase paraffin candles in glass bases that will burn for 100 hours each. They sell for about $4 and are available from *Emergency Essentials* and other preparedness stores.

The advantage of candles is that they are relatively inexpensive and easy to store. Whenever we find a good sale on candles, we stock up. The disadvantage is that they can tip over easily and cause a fire. Purchasing candle holders with a central spike will reduce the chance of the candle falling out of the holder. Also, never put a candle in a wooden holder - the holder can catch fire. The best candle holders are made of metal or glass and leave plenty of space around the base of the candle. Particularly if you have children, never leave a burning candle unattended. Either blow out the candle before you leave the room, or take it with you. It's good practice to start burning candles regularly as soon as you read this book. That way, you and your family will become accustomed to remembering to blow them out before bed, and to keeping an eye on them while they are burning.

Another alternative for lighting within a room is the old-fashioned oil lamp. These burn basic cooking oil. They are usually less expensive than kerosene lamps, but tend to give off a smelly, sooty smoke. *Lehman's* in Kidron, Ohio, sells inexpensive adapters for between $4 and $5 that will enable you to convert mason jars or wine bottles into oil lamps. If you decide to use an oil lamp for light, be sure you store enough oil for both cooking and lighting.

Kerosene lamps are similar to oil lamps: glass bases, metal burners, wide cotton wicks, and chimneys. In general, the cleaner burning lamps are the more expensive ones. The pricier lamps also tend to produce more light. They burn either kerosene or paraffin lamp oil. When buying a lamp, be sure to determine how long it will burn with a base full of fuel. The best we found in this category is the Aladdin lamp. It uses a wick and a mantle, and generates up to 60 watts of light. When you purchase an oil lamp, it is a good idea to buy replacement parts including a glass chimney, and some spare wicks, and mantles. Lamps and fuel can be purchased at antique stores, preparedness stores, department and discount stores, or through mail order from *Lehman's*. See instructions in *Chapter 5* for catalog information, or visit them on-line at

Chapter 6 — Light, Heat, Washing, and Waste

www.Lehmans.com. A caution: if you have small children, you should not buy glass lamps unless you plan to mount them on the wall. If they are knocked over, the glass can break and start a fire.

Another alternative is a type of flashlight with a pop-up middle that converts the device into a battery-powered light that can sit on a table. They don't provide as much light as an Aladdin lamp, but can serve as an alternative to candles or oil lamps. These can be found in either camping supply or home improvement stores.

Speaking of flashlights, Al found the flashlight to beat all at the Denver Preparedness Expo. It is called the StarLight™. The flashlight is powered by a powerful magnet, and will never need batteries or light bulbs. To recharge the light, you simply shake the flashlight. Only one minute of shaking provides more than five minutes of light. We don't know how we ever lived without one. The flashlight is a little pricey, retailing at nearly $100. However, it's functionality is unbeatable. To order, visit their website at www.innovativetech.org, or call (800) 696-7051.

Out-of-doors activities will probably be kept to a minimum after dark, but if you need to go out, you'll want higher powered flashlights, or sturdy kerosene lanterns designed for camping. Many different models are available in home improvement and hardware stores, discount stores, and from companies who sell camping supplies. With outdoor lanterns, durability is important, so carefully inspect and compare lanterns in different price ranges and styles before purchasing one.

If the electricity goes off in your neighborhood, streetlights obviously will not function, and it will be extremely dark outside. You may want to consider installing solar powered or battery powered exterior lights. They come in many sizes and styles, and can either be mounted on the side of your house, or stuck into the ground. The effectiveness of solar powered lights will vary depending on how many hours of sunlight and the amount of cloud cover you receive each day. During the winter months, solar may not be the best option. Some lights will come on automatically at dusk; others will turn on only if they sense motion nearby. Before deciding what to purchase, you'll want to know how long the light will last on a single solar charge or with new batteries. Also consider the amount of light each type gives off. Exterior lights can be found in home improvement and hardware stores.

Shelter from The Cold

The bad news is that January 1, 2000 will occur in the middle of winter. The good news is that we live in an age of technologically advanced home products and clothing, both of which can help keep us warm. If you live in a place where it is not cold or raining or snowing, you will probably be much more concerned about finding water than heating your home. But, for the majority of us in the United States, warmth will be an important issue.

As we thought about lighting and heating our home, we realized that the best plan would be to select a room or two to be our main living area during an electrical outage. Because we live in a single story brick house with a basement, we will spend time during the day in our upstairs family room, unless it is extremely cold. Then, at night, we will move down to the basement, which tends to be warmer than the upper level in the winter. If you live in a multi-story house with cathedral ceilings and a basement, you may find it easier to heat and use your basement full time instead of using a room on the main level. An advantage to a basement is that it can be cozier and warmer. A disadvantage is that supplies and wastewater must be carried up and down the stairs. Take into consideration the amount of sun you receive in various rooms of your house, the quality of ventilation, and the amount of space available. If you are able to burn wood and have a wood stove in your home, the room where the stove is located will probably be the place you congregate most frequently.

Chapter 6   *Light, Heat, Washing, and Waste*

The Olsen's first heating priorities were insulating our home and our bodies first, before worrying about how to generate heat artificially. Depending on where you live, how cold it gets, and what type of construction your home is, your needs will vary.

If you already live in a cold or snowy climate, keeping your body warm should require only minimal extra preparedness. If you need to buy new blankets and clothing, you can take advantage of innovations in garment and fabric design. We stocked up on various weights of long underwear, turtlenecks, sweat pants and sweat shirts for our family. Garments designed to wear after skiing, such as polypropylene pants are also great for indoor and outdoor use during cold spells. The idea is to wear lots of layers and have enough changes of the bottom layer next to your skin - socks and long underwear, so that these can be freshly clean every day. Once a garment has been worn and perspired in, its ability to keep you warm is diminished.

Since keeping the head and feet warm helps retain body heat, we also invested in some soft, lightweight ski caps and rag wool socks. We can wear them around the house, and while sleeping. We also splurged on some toasty down booties for wearing inside. If you live in a climate where it snows in the winter, snow plows might not be operating in your neighborhood for a while. Warm, weatherproof snow boots, high enough for deep snow, may be a wise investment. Al thinks we should outfit the entire family in showshoes. Although they are a little bit lower on the priority list, we are considering it.

The easiest way to retain heat in your home is to add insulation. Insulation prices and effectiveness vary depending on the quality, the material used, and the density of the material. You can add insulation to your attic, ceiling, interior and exterior walls, and windows. The degree to which insulation helps retain heat will vary depending on the design, size, and layout of your home; the materials your home is constructed with; and the climate you live in. You may want to consider insulating your main living rooms, and closing off other rooms during an emergency. Be sure to insulate windows in the rooms you plan to spend time in. Windows account for up to half of the heat loss in a building.

Window insulation effectiveness can be evaluated through R-value (measuring resistance to heat flow) and/or the U-value (measuring conductance of heat). Windows with high R-values lose less heat than ones with lower R-values. The opposite is true with U-values. Typically, R-values range from 0.9 to 3.0, and U-values range from 1.1 to 0.3. To determine your windows' energy efficiency, consider the frame as well as the window itself.

There are any number of ways you can insulate windows, including weather-stripping and caulking frames; installing coatings or film to reduce heat transfer; installing energy efficient glass; replacing frames with energy efficient material; or by increasing the number of layers of glass through magnetic interior inserts or exterior storm windows. Heat loss can also be minimized by using thermal window coverings or shades inside the house. If you add additional layers of glass, be sure you can still receive air through an open window to provide proper ventilation for burning your heater or cooking stove.

When contemplating adding insulation to your home, consult an expert and research various options before deciding which best fits your particular situation. Refer to the source table at the end of the chapter for information on insulation methods and products.

One other strategy for keeping warm overnight is to sleep in a camping tent inside your house. You can also sleep next to another person, or with an animal. Ben has his own two-person tent that fits in his bedroom. He has had such a great time sleeping in his tent during our preparedness weekends, that he wants to keep the tent up and sleep in it for the rest of the

Chapter 6 — Light, Heat, Washing, and Waste

winter. Katie loves to sleep with her dog. On a good day, when Ben and Katie like each other and aren't engaged in normal sibling spats, both kids and the dog sleep cozily in the tent.

Generating heat inside your home without the benefit of electricity or natural gas can be tricky. If you are able to store and burn wood, and wood is accessible and reasonably priced in your area, you may want to consider installing a wood burning stove. If you have a wood burning fireplace, installing a wood stove inside it will increase the heat output dramatically. Depending on how much money and space you have, you can either get a wood heating stove or a wood cooking stove. Another option is to install solid fitting glass doors and a metal fireback in your fireplace to increase heat production. Check with your home builder or wood stove dealer to determine your most suitable solutions.

If you decide to burn wood, a rule of thumb is that harder woods, such as oak or walnut, burn hotter. Pine tends to catch fire and burn easily, but a residue of burnt pine "pitch" can build up in a stove or chimney and be a fire hazard. Also, when chopping wood, be sure to wear steel-toed boots and safety goggles. For more information about burning wood for heat and making your fireplace produce more heat, see *James Dulley* in the source list at the end of the chapter.

Due to air pollution guidelines and space limitations, many of us will not be able to burn wood to heat our homes. A natural way to produce heat if you live in a climate with winter sunshine is to build a solar window heater. You can also build a solar water heater. The materials needed are relatively inexpensive. Plans and material lists are available from *James Dulley*.

Al discovered a product called Alco Brite ® that can be burned for heating. Alco Brite ® is a gelled ethanol fuel that can be used safely in confined areas. It is packaged in heavy duty steel cans, and is advertised to have an indefinite shelf life. One 16-ounce can burns for about 4 hours and produces approximately 2,500 BTU's of heat per hour. The price is approximately $3 per can. Alco Brite ® sells portable fireplaces which don't require a chimney, vent, or flue. They also make inserts for existing wood burning fireplaces. For around $200, you can get the insert and artificial logs to camouflage the fuel cans. If you don't have a fireplace at all, Alco Brite ® sells a free standing fireplace in a wooden console, which retails between $500 and $875, depending on what type of cabinet you choose. We discovered that Alco Brite ® fuel can be burned in a portable fireplace that sells for between $65 and $80 in catalogs or camping supply stores. See the resource table at the end of the chapter for information on how to order Alco Brite ®. The product can be purchased from the manufacturer or at selected preparedness stores. If you decide to use a portable fireplace inside, do not burn wood in it. Portable fireplaces do not have proper ventilation for wood burning.

Garbage In - Garbage Out

For me, this could be the worst part of living with a disrupted utility grid. Sanitation is one area that will be severely impacted if you do not have a yard. Urban dwellers will have to carry garbage and other waste to the street in plastic bags, and anyone who has ever survived a big city garbage strike will know just how quickly the situation becomes really unpleasant if trucks aren't coming by to remove it. If you live in a city, do not wait to find out whether local sanitation officials have a plan in case of a grid failure. Find out now. If there is no plan in place, you will need to be resourceful in making your own. Perhaps there is a common area outdoors near your home where it will be possible to dig holes for waste and water disposal. Many buildings have communal basement spaces where recyclable may be gathered and held until pick-up resumes. Some buildings still have furnaces that may offer a way to dispose of burnable material. A last resort for short-term emergency garbage holding may be covered receptacles placed on the roof of your building.

Chapter 6 — Light, Heat, Washing, and Waste

During our preparedness weekends, we rehearsed with a modified sanitation situation. We permitted ourselves the use of conventional toilets, but not the use of running water or drains in the sinks or bathtubs. This helped us learn how to heat, conserve, transport, and dispose of water. We also agreed not to use the garbage disposal or our traditional trash system. Learning how much waste paper and food packaging we generate each day was appalling.

To dispose of paper waste, Al found an old 55-gallon metal drum at a swap meet. We will use it to burn things like paper towels, can and jar labels, cereal boxes, etc. For other packaging waste such as cans, we'll rinse them out with rain water; remove tops, bottoms and labels; and flatten the centers. Then they will be buried in another hole in the backyard that we've reserved for trash. This hole is close to our waste water pit. We decided to dig it before the ground froze, just in case garbage removal is disrupted for longer than a month. Al and Ben dug a hole three feet square and four feet deep, and put all of the dirt in plastic trash barrels in the garage. All trash that can't be burned or reused will be buried in this hole in plastic trash bags, and periodically filled over with the saved loose dirt. The hole will be covered with a tarp anchored by bricks or large rocks to prevent snow and rain from filling it up, and to keep Cisco out of it. During weekend drills, we're not burning in the drum yet because it is against the law. We are not burying trash either, but we are becoming more conscious of ways we can reduce the amount and the size of trash that we give to garbage haulers each week.

If you are a man, skip this paragraph. If you are a woman, you'll definitely want to read it. One of the neatest new products we've discovered in our preparedness research is a feminine hygiene product called "The Keeper™." The product is a rubber cup about 2 inches long that effectively replaces a tampon. It can be re-used for several years, is reasonably priced, and comes with a money back guarantee. After using this product, I must say I'm a convert. I like it because it is effective, convenient, and good for the environment. The company who makes it also has recently come out with washable external feminine protection that resembles a sanitary napkin, only made out of cloth. For more information on either product, call 1-888-882-1818.

Cleaning Up the Kitchen

We've already discussed having a large kettle or enamel pot available for heating water. If you have a choice, water for washing should not be taken from your drinking water barrels. Rainwater or melted snow can be heated for washing.

For dish detail after meals, we use two separate dish pans. For washing, we use water that we've saved from a previous meal's rinse water. We reheat it on our camp stove in a large enamel pot, and pour it into the first dishpan. In the second, we pour fresh boiling water, then add a small amount of cooler water for rinsing. Wearing rubber gloves allows us to use hotter water to wash and rinse our dishes. To keep the water as clean and re-usable as possible, we use rubber scrapers to get every bit of food out of pots and pans and off our plates before washing - - organic (fruit and vegetable) scraps get scraped into a plastic bucket that will eventually be dumped onto our compost pile outside; protein, fat, and starch scraps go into Cisco's bowl and magically disappear.

Non-polluting liquid detergent, and other environmentally friendly cleaning products, are available at health food stores, and from local distributors of *Shaklee* and *Amway*. To prevent contamination of your yard and our planet, we strongly recommend using non-toxic cleaning products. Many of these cleaning agents are concentrated and multi-purpose, so you can use them to clean dishes, surfaces, and clothing.

Chapter 6 — Light, Heat, Washing, and Waste

After the dishes have been washed and rinsed, the fairly clean rinse water is saved in the enamel pot to be used as the next meal's wash water. Then, the washing water is strained through the grease trap in the back yard, and poured into the wastewater hole.

When we started trying to live without running water, we found that we needed more receptacles for transporting, heating, and storing water. You can try this yourself and see what works best for you and the space you live in.

If your home has a yard, we recommend you dig holes before the ground freezes. You will need one hole for waste water generated by washing. In his book, *The Sense of Survival* (Orem, Utah, Timpanogos Publishers, 1990), J. Allan South recommends digging a hole two feet deep and four feet square, and lining the bottom with rocks or gravel. If waste water contains grease, he recommends straining it through a grease filter made out of a bucket with holes in the bottom. South advises filling the bottom six or eight inches of the bucket with gravel, and then putting sand or wood ashes for the top twelve inches. Burlap can also be placed at the top of the bucket. This prevents the waste water hole from becoming clogged with grease.

If you live five flights up on the top floor of a Victorian in San Francisco, as Anne used to, hauling used washing water down to ground level instead of dumping it out the window will be kinder to your neighbors. You might consider pouring old dish water into a five gallon plastic bucket, and taking it down when it has a few gallons of water in it. Remember, water weighs eight pounds per gallon.

Life Without the Loo

Now let's talk about all of that icky bathroom stuff. First of all, we recommend you dig a hole for an outhouse. When we were kids up at the cabin, our grandparents had a two-seater outhouse that was named "Pink Pearl." It was painted pink inside and out. I always wondered why it had two seats, and now I know. It is much less frightening to visit the outhouse with another person, when you are a kid, than it is to go by yourself. I used to go out there with my grandma all of the time. If your family is fairly shy about running around without clothing and going to the bathroom in private, you may be making a few adjustments.

J. Allan South (*The Sense of Survival*) suggests digging a hole four to six feet deep and two feet square per seat for the outhouse and building a wooden toilet box. Per Mr. South, toilet boxes should be sixteen inches tall, with elliptical shaped holes on top that are nine inches wide and twelve inches long. The box should be mounted on a solid base that surrounds the hole to prevent the box from collapsing or falling in the hole. Wooden toilet seats with lids can be mounted on the toilet box. Lids help reduce pest infestation and odor. South recommends spraying the inside of the outhouse with insecticide.

An outhouse hole should be dug before the ground freezes, and be sure to place it far away from water retention cisterns or wells, and facing east if possible to take advantage of morning sun warmth. We put ours outside of the door that leads from the rear of our garage to our back yard. In her book, *Homesteading Adventures: A Guide for Doers and Dreamers*, (ManyTracks Publishing, 1997), Sue Robishaw explains that you can use a tent around a toilet box seat for a temporary outhouse instead of building a wooden structure. If you decide to build a wooden outhouse, Sue Robishaw suggests installing a window in the back and a loose fitting door. You will also want to dump ashes, dirt, sawdust, and/or lime into the hole periodically to minimize pests and odor. We have not yet built our outhouse. We plan to build it in September of 1999. Once it is in place, we will start using it one weekend a month when we have preparedness drills.

Chapter 6   Light, Heat, Washing, and Waste

We strongly suggest investing in a portable potty to minimize trips outside in the middle of the night, or during freezing cold weather. They are fairly inexpensive and are available at preparedness stores. We have a policy in our house that whoever uses it will empty (except Katie), rinse the receptacle out with water from our outside trough, and spray with diluted all-purpose cleaner. If you don't want to build an outhouse or outdoor toilet box, you can use a portable toilet exclusively and empty it into a hole dug specifically to dispense with human waste. Then you can shovel dirt, sawdust, etc. into the hole every time you dump waste into it.

For hand washing, we try to use warm dish washing water whenever possible. Everyone in the family is encouraged to use the bathroom right after a meal, if they need to, so they can wash their hands in the dish washing water. We also pour some hot water into a pitcher, and everyone takes turns using a wash basin for hand and face washing or limited body washing. For brushing teeth, we get water from our drinking water cooler. Whenever possible, we brush our teeth outside over the wastewater pit. If it is too cold outside, we rinse into the compost bucket.

Low-Tech Laundry

The first rule of laundry in our house is - the less the better. Living without electricity will also mean washing clothes by hand. So, the first thing we will do to minimize our wash loads is to change clothes more often. If we are doing dirty work, we'll wear work clothes, and for cleaner work, we'll change. I've learned to wear an apron in the kitchen to keep my clothes cleaner while cooking and hauling and heating water. Socks and underwear are the only things we will change daily during an emergency.

How sophisticated your laundry system is will depend largely on how much money you have to spend. We decided to get two big galvanized steel tubs, one for washing, and one for rinsing. We also purchased a really cool tool for about $10 from *Lehman's* that looks like a plumber's plunger. It has a spring on the end, and when plunged through a tub full of clothes, water, and soap, cleans clothes rather well. We also got an old fashioned washboard from *Lehman's*. If you have $130 or so, you can purchase a hand wringer. Preparedness and camping supply stores sell portable washers for about $50 that use a hand crank and an enclosed cylinder to clean clothing.

We decided to save money and use mostly elbow grease for our laundry. When lots of people help, laundry is much easier to do. In our house, the whole family contributes. Funny thing, when everyone does their part of the laundry chore, the amount of dirty laundry lessens dramatically.

It is best to wash clothes in the middle of the afternoon when the temperature is warmest. Heat hot water and pour it in equal amounts into the washing and rinsing tubs, then add small amounts of cooler water and stir with your hands until you have the temperature you want. We have learned not to overfill these tubs, because they are a bear to empty if they get too heavy. We then add a small amount of liquid, non-polluting laundry cleaner. I am in charge of plunging and scrubbing. Ben rinses. Al wrings and stacks the clothes in a laundry basket. Then, we dump out the first rinse water and refill the tub with clean water. Ben rinses again. Al does the final wringing. The larger and stronger your hands are, the better job you do of manually wringing clothes. Katie helps smooth out the clothing which is then hung on a clothesline we made in our basement, or from plastic hangers on a steel pipe. If you don't have a place to suspend clothes in your house, you can purchase drying racks from catalogs, hardware stores, or discount stores.

Since we often have 60 degree days with sunshine during the winter in Colorado, Al will construct an outdoor clothesline. He has all of the necessary parts, but won't put it up until late in the year,

Chapter 6 — Light, Heat, Washing, and Waste

because our neighborhood convenants don't allow clotheslines. We are currently working to change these rules to permit clotheslines and outhouses.

Functioning without electricity one weekend a month has really helped us appreciate the art of housekeeping that our grandmothers practiced. At first, we were overwhelmed with the amount of labor and time involved in keeping our living environment clean. As time passes, we become more skilled at managing the situation. This may sound strange, but pitching in with the other members of our family to learn, and to get the work done, has done wonders for our relationships, and made us feel more connected. We've actually had fun working together and finding new ways to adapt to thriving without modern conveniences. Our children have also matured, learning to think creatively, and to work hard. In *Chapter 7*, we will show you how to stage a back-to-basics weekend, and recap the important lessons from this book.

Light, Heat, Washing, and Waste Supplies - Mail Order Sources

Item	Source	Contact Information	✓
Gelled Ethanol Fuel and Free Standing Fireplaces	*Alco Brite ®*	(800) 473-0717 PO Box 840926 Hildale, UT 84784	
Oil Lamps and Lanterns	*Cumberland General Store*	www.cumberlandgeneral.com or Send $4 for Catalog to: #1 Highway 68 Crossville, TN 38555 (800) 334-4640	
	Lehman's Non-Electric Catalog	www.Lehmans.com or send $3 for catalog to: Lehman's PO Box 41 Kidron, Ohio 44636 (330) 857-5757	
Outdoor Solar Lights and Solar Heating Information	*James Dulley*	www.dulley.com or write to: PO Box 54987 Cincinnati, OH 45254 for Update Bulletin Listing (send self-addressed business sized envelope)	
Information and/or Purchase	*Jade Mountain*	www.jademountain.com (800) 442-1972 PO Box 4616 Boulder, CO 80306-4616	
	Real Goods	www.realgoods.com (800) 762-7325 555 Leslie Street Ukiah, CA 95482-5576	
Home Insulation Information	*Center for Renewable Energy & Sustainable Technology*	www.solstice.crest.org 350 Townsend St., Suite 100 San Francisco, CA 94107 (415) 284-6400	
	James Dulley	www.dulley.com or write to: (see above)	
	The Energy Efficiency and Renewable Energy Clearinghouse	PO Box 3048 Merrifield, VA 22116 (800) 363-3732	
	US Department of Energy Energy Efficiency and Renewable Energy Network (EREN)	www.eren.doe.gov	
Washtubs	*Cumberland General Store*	www.cumberlandgeneral.com (see above)	
	Lehman's	www.Lehmans.com (see above)	

Disclaimer: *This list was compiled for your convenience. It does not guarantee the availability or quality of products or suppliers, nor is it a complete list of potential suppliers. As information changes over time, this list may not be accurate. Conduct your own research before purchasing products.*

Light and Heat Action Plan

✓ To Do	Activity	Person Responsible	Due Date	✓ Done
	Lighting Supplies			
	Candles			
	Candle Holders			
	Matches			
	Flashlights			
	Batteries			
	Fire Extinguisher			
	Smoke Detectors			
	Optional Lighting			
	Outdoor Lights			
	Outdoor Lantern			
	Headlamp			
	Oil Lamp			
	Aladdin Lamp			
	Replacement Parts			
	Lamp Fuel			
	Heating			
	Smoke Detector			
	Heater or Stove			
	Heating Fuel			
	Clothing and Blankets:			
	Optional Heating			
	Window Insulation			
	Thermal Coverings			
	Wall Insulation			
	Solar Window Heater			
	Backup Heater			
	Fuel for Backup			
	Tent			

Washing and Waste Action Plan

✓ To Do	Activity	Person Responsible	Due Date	✓ Done
	Dish Washing Supplies			
	Dish Washing Pan			
	Dish Rinsing Pan			
	Water Bucket			
	Organic Dish Soap			
	Rubber Gloves			
	Sponges/Dish Rags			
	Dish Drainer			
	Enamel Pot			
	Garbage			
	Burning Receptacle			
	Dig Garbage Hole			
	Wastewater Pit			
	Grease Filter			
	Compost Bin			
	Laundry			
	Large Washing Bin			
	Large Rinsing Bin			
	Organic Detergent			
	Clothesline			
	Clothespins			
	Laundry Optional			
	Laundry Plunger			
	Washboard			
	Drying Rack			
	Hand Wringer			
	Personal Hygiene			
	Wash Basin			
	Tub for Baths			
	Portable Toilet			
	Outdoor Toilet Box			
	Tent w/out Floor			
	Outhouse or Shed			
	Sawdust/Lime			
	Waste Disposal Pit			
	Camp Shower			

Light, Heat, Washing, Waste Blank Action Plan

✓ To Do	Activity	Person Responsible	Due Date	✓ Done

I signify that the Light, Heat, Washing, and Waste Preparedness Activities are complete. Our Household Has Successfully Taken Action to Prepare for a Grid Failure or Natural Disaster

_____
Signed

_____
Date

Taking Action

It's a Saturday morning in September. The house is silent. Cool, barely-autumn air seeps through the open bedroom window. Drifting in that wonderful place between asleep and awake, I imagine that someone is nibbling on my ear. I roll over and open one eye. Al winks at me. Reality sinks in. The kids spent the night at Anne's. Today is a bonus day.

In the kitchen, Al serves me coffee, we pop some bagels in the toaster and share the paper in silence. Today represents the calm before the storm. Next week our book will be released. We've just begun selling copies to people we know. It seems like Y2K has taken over our lives.

Even our kids are becoming entrenched. Last night, we packed up Ben's tent and some sleeping bags, and they went over to Aunt Annie's house to bake cookies in a camp oven, read pioneer stories, and sleep in a tent in her living room. Our kids - the former televisionaholics. Now, they think it is more fun to play board games, use candlelight, and read stories aloud. They've even asked if they can invite their friends over during our back-to-basics weekends. When we started this, we never anticipated that our children would have this reaction.

We've learned a great deal about ourselves and our world during the last six months. Some good news, some bad news. The good news is that we are more innovative and flexible than we thought. We know now that anyone who is determined can adapt to the challenges of the new millennium. Adapting is our country's core competency. We also discovered how lucky we are to have products, technologies, and tools available to us that our ancestors didn't have. Overall, what we've learned by doing the research, meeting with people, and preparing our own household for the Year 2000, is that it isn't as complicated as we thought it would be.

Chapter 7   Taking Action

The bad news is that we still see some of our own families and friends ignoring our warnings, continuing to spend money on frills instead of on preparedness. They can't seem to find the time to buy some extra food and water storage barrels, even though we've given them the information on how to do so. They are so busy feeding the machines that are their modern lifestyles, just like mice running on spinning wheels. We hope that our book will help them take action.

If you are reading this chapter, then hopefully you've begun working on your action plans, or you may even be finished. Congratulations! If you haven't started, then just do one simple thing - document your battery inventory or order some water barrels. You will be amazed at how each small step generates momentum and propels you closer to preparedness. It's kind of like having a baby or getting a master's degree. If you wait until you have the time or the money, you'll never do it.

How to Stage a Back-to-Basics Weekend

Disclaimer: *Stage a back-to-basics weekend at your own risk. The author assumes no liability for incidents or injury which may occur as a result of use or misuse of this information.*

Once you have a water storage barrel, a camp stove and some fuel, a fire extinguisher, some candles and/or an oil lamp, an alternative heat source, and some pans to heat water and food in (Ideally, you will have completed all of your Level 1 preparedness activities listed in the action plans) - then you are ready to stage a back-to-basics weekend.

We have a few suggestions. First of all, if it is in the middle of winter, choose a weekend that is forecast to be warmer than normal. You will have a better chance of success if you aren't dealing with bitter weather your first time out of the chute. Also, start with a back-to-basics night. Saturday is good for your first one - you'll have more time during the day to prepare. Make a list of food, clothing, and supplies you will need. Make sure you know where they are located. Agree on the goals and the ground rules, write them down, and stick to them.
Goals for the Olsen family weekends:

> *The Olsen family is completely committed to preparing for a potential grid failure or natural disaster. Therefore, we will host back-to-basics weekends every month. The goal will be to replicate the actual situations we may face during an emergency so that we can adapt, anticipate, and prepare - both our environment, and ourselves. We believe that the lessons we learn today will enable us to be more self-sufficient and satisfied, and to help others in the future.*

Writing your own goal statement is a positive thing to do. It makes the exercise real, and helps your household team focus on results. Take the time now and write a goal statement for your back-to-basics weekends. Read it at the beginning of each weekend, and display it during each exercise.

Next, you will want to create your own ground rules. They will vary depending on the priorities and personalities of the members of your household. You can use ours as an example.

1. The Olsen family will hold back-to-basics weekends for at least one weekend per month, every month.
2. The weekend will officially commence at 5:00 p.m. on Friday, and terminate at 8:00 p.m. on Sunday.
3. Every member of the family will assume equal responsibility for the success of the exercise.

Chapter 7 Taking Action

4. Al Olsen will be in charge of preparing the house by turning off all power breakers except for the refrigerator and the hot water heater. He will also cause faucets on outside walls to drip so the pipes will not freeze in the winter. It will be his responsibility to make sure the house is safe and stable during the exercise. He will supervise the use of tools and non-electrical implements. He will return the environment to normal on Sunday.
5. Nancy Olsen will be in charge of meal planning and food and water management.
6. Ben Olsen will be in charge of garbage management and dog management. He will help haul water, use the grease filter, flatten cans, and burn trash. He will make sure Cisco is fed and has fresh water.
7. Katie Olsen will be in charge of entertainment and morale. She will gather games, books, musical instruments, and crafts, and be responsible for keeping track of all the pieces and leading the clean up effort after recreational activities.
8. Cisco Olsen will be in charge of consuming non-compostable leftovers and will serve as a bathroom companion, when needed. He will also be in charge of security.
9. Anne Wright (a.k.a. Aunt Annie) will be in charge of planning each weekend. Every weekend will have a different educational and experiential theme emphasis such as using solar energy, laundry without electricity, or cooking with a pressure cooker. Anne will also write an evaluation at the conclusion of each weekend and outline areas of success and goals for improvement at the beginning of the next back-to-basics weekend. She will make lists of any items which need to be added to our preparedness inventory.
10. Indoor toilets are the only modern convenience that may be used during the exercise. Beginning in late 1999, an outhouse and portable toilet will be used. The use of electric lights, running water, the refrigerator, the heater, radios, television, and the telephone are prohibited.
11. Unless a life or death medical emergency occurs, the family agrees not to use any outside services such as grocery stores, restaurants, etc. during the weekend. The family may use neighbors as resources, and may borrow non-electrical necessities from neighbors.
12. Recognizing that modern life will go on during the back-to-basics weekends, recreational activities and automobile usage will be limited to activities involving a regular commitment - such as playing on sports teams, taking piano lessons, or attending church services. Neighborhood recreation is allowed as long as all chores have been completed and the recreation does not involve electricity. Non-essential activities will be scheduled for another weekend.

Anne wrote out a list of possible back-to-basics weekend themes.

⇒ Fire safety - lamps, candles, and stoves
⇒ Cooking with a pressure cooker
⇒ Snowshoeing
⇒ Finding, hauling, purifying, and managing water
⇒ Basic first aid
⇒ Battery management and solar recharging
⇒ Laundry without electricity
⇒ Baking bread and tortilla making

Well, you get the idea. Try staging your own back-to-basics weekend. Believe me, by the second or third month, you'll look forward to the adventure, and be amazed at how much you learn and

Chapter 7   *Taking Action*

improve. Our weekends have been so successful that other people in the neighborhood have heard about them, and their kids are pressuring them to try it. We have had neighbors come over for a dinner without electricity, and this has really helped motivate them. Now people are talking about trying to get our whole neighborhood to shut down for one weekend a month, and share ideas, resources, and supplies. It is amazing.

We should emphasize that you need to pace yourself - crawl, walk, and then run. I wouldn't go out to the neighbors and try to organize a back-to-basics weekend block party your first time out. It is kind of like when you are flying in an airplane, and they tell you that if oxygen masks drop, put on your own mask first, then you will be in a position to help the person sitting next to you if they need assistance.

What We've Left Out

You may have noticed that we have not covered a few topics which may be of concern to you and your family. They are - medical needs and physical security. This has been intentional. Originally, we had planned an entire chapter on medical issues. Then, we interviewed a family physician and an MD who also practices eastern (acupuncture) and western medicine. Both of them recommended that families store fairly robust first aid kits, and then suggested that having access to clean drinking water and food would be much more important than worrying about medical issues that might arise. As we've said before, if you have a medical condition that requires special medication or electrical devices, consult with your physician and determine what action you can take to protect yourself. It is a good idea to obtain copies of family medical records for your personal files in case computerized records are inaccessible.

Obviously, you can prepare for potentially having limited access to doctors or medical help by doing a few things, today. First of all, take care of yourself physically, now. See a dentist regularly. Practice good oral hygiene. Take care of any potentially long term medical issues you might have. If you need elective surgery and have been putting it off - schedule it. If you have a physical ailment or symptoms that have been annoying you - see a doctor and have them checked out immediately. Also, if you wear glasses to see, be sure you have a current prescription and a spare pair of sturdy glasses.

If the utility grid is impaired, you can expect that people trained in medicine will be working mostly on emergencies. It is a good idea to find out what skills the people who live on your block may have. In exchange for medical help in the future, you may want to donate preparedness supplies now to families or individuals with special skills. It is critical that anyone who has medical skills or anyone who works for a public utility provider make sure that their household is prepared as well as possible, so they will feel secure going to work and leaving their families in the event of an emergency.

You can also learn how to treat many ailments and injuries yourself. In Chapter 2, we suggested taking a class from The School of Natural Healing. For course information, call 1-800-372-8255.

As far as personal security is concerned, we've had many people talk to us about guns. Some people have said that it doesn't matter if they are prepared. They think that if they have supplies, people will bring guns to their homes to take whatever they have.

The reason we wrote this book is because we firmly believe that if you prepare your family at least at Level 1, and if you help your neighbors who live on each side of you prepare, the use of guns to take food from other people is far less likely to occur. We don't even want to consider going to our neighbor's house, pointing a loaded gun at them, and demanding food or water. We can't

Chapter 7 — Taking Action

imagine anyone who wants to be in that situation. Having a gun in your home for personal protection is up to you. If you decide to purchase a firearm, take a hunter safety course, and lock it unloaded in a gun safe. Enough said.

If you have food and water, and your neighbors have food and water - as much as you can find the money and space for, then you have Year 2000 insurance. You will buy time for the people who will be called on to deal with or repair any disruptions in our infrastructure. We sincerely believe that if everyone takes the time to consider what might happen, and to realize that no one really knows what *will* happen, they will absolutely take action, now!

Year 2000 Final Action Plan

Activity	Date Completed	✓
Complete General Household Action Plan		
Complete Food Storage Action Plan		
Complete Water Action Plan		
Complete Food Preparation Action Plan		
Complete Light, Heat, Washing and Waste Action Plan		
Stage a Back-to-Basics Evening		
Stage a Back-to-Basics Weekend		
Stage a Back-to-Basics Weekend		
Stage a Back-to-Basics Weekend		
Stage a Back-to-Basics Weekend		
Stage a Back-to-Basics Weekend		
Work with Next Door Neighbors on Preparedness		

We signify that the Year 2000 Action Plans are complete.
Our Household Is Prepared for a Grid Failure or Natural Disaster

_____
Signed

_____
Signed

_____
Signed

_____
Signed

_____
Date

Index

—A—

Aerobic oxygen, 97

—B—

Back-to-basics weekend, 122, 133
    goals, 134
    rules, 134
Bathroom
    supplies, 33
Battery
    inventory, 45
Budget
    bathroom supplies, 33
    battery inventory, 45
    electronic device replacement, 41
    first aid kit, 37
    food, 69
    games and entertainment, 49
    kitchen supply, 29

—C—

Cabela's, 111
Candle
    holders, 117
    safety, 116, 117
Candles
    advantages, 117
    burn time, 117
    disadvantage, 117
Canning. *See also food preservation methods*
    pressure canning, 109
    water bath, 109
Carbon monoxide, 105
Cast Iron Cookware
    mail order suppliers, 111
Christian Family Resources, 85
Country Store Preparedness Center, The, 85, 98
Cookbooks, 103
Cooking
    on two burner stove, 104
Cooking fuel
    conserving, 107
    propane, 106
Cookware
    cast iron, 107
    cast iron griddle, 107
    Dutch oven, 107
    pressure cookers, 107
    woks, 107
Cumberland General Store, 111

—D—

Dehydration, 109
Dulley, James, 111

—E—

Ecology Action, 91
Electricity
    living without, 106
Electronic Devices
    replacement, 41
Emergency Essentials, 85, 117
Emery, Carla, 106
Evangelista, Anita, 106

—F—

Fire extinguisher, 105
First Aid Kit, 37
Flashlight
    battery life, 117
    head lamps, 117
    Starlight flashlight, 118
Flour
    grinding your own, 109
Food
    basics, 57
    bulk, 57
    bulk buying, 69
    discounts, 58
    planning, 56
    shopping list, 65
Food For Thought of Montana, 85
Food packaging
    5 gallon buckets, 57
    number 10 cans, 57
Food planning
    budget, 57
Food preparation
    mail order supply sources, 111
Food preservation methods
    canning, 109
    dehydration, 109
    root cellaring, 109
Food storage
    books, 90
    Do's and Don'ts, 70
    finding space for, 70
Forever Foods, 85

—G—

Games
    inventory, 49
Gardening, 91

books on, 91
Grains
   whole, 91
Grinding
   grain mills, 109
Grocery store
   living without, 57

—H—

Happy Hovel Storable Foods, 85
H&W Distributors, 85, 98
Heat
   sources, 118
   without fireplace, 120
   wood burning, 119
Heater
   solar, 120
High Country Gourmet, 85
Honey
   benefits of, 89

—I—

Insulation
   benefits, 118
   planning, 119, 125
   window, 119
Inventory
   bathroom supplies, 33
   kitchen supplies, 31

—J—

Jade Mountain, 98, 111, 125
Jeavons, John, 91

—K—

Kansas Wind Power, 111
Keeper, The, 121
Kitchen
   supplies, 29

—L—

Lakeridge Food Storage, 85
Lamps
   Aladdin, 115, 117
   mail order sources, 125
   oil, 116, 117
Lanterns
   outdoor, 118
Laundry
   without electricity, 123
Layton, Peggy, 56, 103
Leftover food
   composting, 104
   managing, 104
Leftovers, 69, 108

Lehman's, 108, 111, 117, 123
Lehman's Non-Electric Catalog, 111
Level 1
   explanation of, 16
   food basics, 57
   food preparation, 113
   water basics preparation, 99
Level 2
   explanation of, 16
   water basics preparation, 99
Level 3
   explanation of, 16
   water basics preparation, 99
Lights
   outdoor, 118
Lillian Vernon catalog, 103

—M—

Menu
   planning, 58, 73
Millennium bug, 14
Millennium Gourmet Food Reserves, 85
Modern Farm, 111
Mountain Magic, 85, 98

—N—

Noah's Pantry, 85

—O—

Outhouse
   building instructions, 122
Ovens
   camping, 106
   Dutch oven, 107
   solar, 106

—R—

Real Goods, 111
Ready Made Resources, 85, 98
Refrigerator
   living without, 108
REI, 111
River Valley Outfitters, 98
Robishaw, Sue, 122
Rombauer, Irma, 103
Rombauer, Marion Becker, 103
Root cellaring. *See* food preservation methods

—S—

Seeds
   non-hybrid, 91

Solar Food Dryer
   instructions to build, 111
   mail order suppliers, 111

Solar heater
  instructions for building, 125
Solar lights
  mail order sources, 125
Solar Ovens
  mail order suppliers, 111
South, J. Allan, 121, 122
Sprouts
  nutritional value of, 89
Stevens, James Talmage, 89
Storage spaces
  finding, 26
Stoves - non-electric
  buying, 104
  mail order suppliers, 111
  propane, 106
  wood cook stoves, 106
Supplies
  bathroom, 33
  kitchen, 29
Survival Products, 85, 98

—T—

Toilet
  portable, 122

—U—

Utility grid, 15

—W—

Washtubs
  mail order sources, 125

Waste water
  disposal of, 122
Water
  average usage, 93
  conservation, 103, 121, 122
  emergency sources of, 95, 96
  hauling, 96, 103
  home sources of, 96
  minimum daily consumption, 93
  retention, 95
  storage, justification for, 94
  weight of, 93
Water filters, 97
Water purification, 96
  boiling, 97
  chlorine bleach usage, 97
  method analysis, 97
  suppliers, 98
  using aerobic oxygen, 97
  using iodine, 97
Water storage
  capacity planning, 94
  containers, 94, 95
  location, 94
Wheat
  grinding, 109
  grain mills, 109

—Y—

Y2K
  expectations, 26
Year 2000
  risk assessment, 15
Yourdon, Ed, 14

Photograph by Douglas Wells

Susan Robinson is a strategy and technology consultant in the telecommunications industry. She holds a Bachelor of Arts degree in English from Colorado State University, and a Master's degree in Business Administration from the University of Colorado at Boulder. Susan lives in Denver.

Order Form

Whatcha Gonna Do If the Grid Goes Down?

Preparing Your Household For the Year 2000

by Susan Robinson

To Place a Telephone Order
Call 1-877-Y2K-SAGE
Colorado Residents, Please Call (303) 282-0708

Discounts for purchase in select quantities are available for Churches, Non-Profit Organizations, and Y2K Neighborhood Groups

---

Mail Order Form

Ship To:

Name: _____

Address: _____

City: _____ State: _____ Zip: _____

Qty: _____ X $22.95 = Sub Total: _____

\+ Shipping: _____

= Sub Total: _____

\+ Sales Tax*: _____

= Total Due: _____

Shipping Charge $4.00 for first book, $1.00 for each additional book

Credit Card Number _____ Expiration _____ Day Time Telephone _____

(Visa or Mastercard) Name as it appears on card (if different from above) _____

*Sales Tax = Colorado residents in the City and County of Denver, 7.3%; Colorado residents in the following counties: Boulder, Jefferson, Adams, Arapahoe, Douglas, & Highlands Ranch, 3.8%; Colorado residents in counties not listed previously, 3%. Non-Colorado residents, 0%.

Mail Order to: Virtual Sage, PO Box 100008, Denver, CO 80250
Please allow 2 weeks for delivery.